# Library Information Skills and the
# High School English Program

# Library and Information Problem-Solving Skills Series

**Paula Kay Montgomery,**
**Series Editor**

*CUES: Choose, Use, Enjoy, Share: A Model for Educational Enrichment Through the School Library Media Center.* Second Edition. By Phyllis B. Leonard.

*Media Skills for Middle Schools: Strategies for Library Media Specialists and Teachers.* Second Edition. By Lucille W. Van Vliet.

*Library Information Skills and the High School English Program.* Second Edition. By Mary H. Hackman.

*Information Literacy and Information Skills Instruction: Applying Research to Practice in the School Library Media Center.* By Nancy Pickering Thomas.

# Library Information Skills and the High School English Program

**Second Edition**

## Mary H. Hackman

Edited by
Paula Kay Montgomery

1999
Libraries Unlimited, Inc.
Englewood, Colorado

Libraries Unlimited, Inc.
P.O. Box 6633
Englewood, CO 80155-6633
1-800-237-6124
www.lu.com


*Production Editor:* Kay Mariea
*Copy Editor:* Louise Tonneson Rodriguez
*Proofreader:* Teri Keeler
*Indexer:* Kay Dusheck
*Typesetter:* Michael Florman

---

**Library of Congress Cataloging-in-Publication Data**

Hackman, Mary H., 1931-
    Library information skills and the high school English program /
Mary H. Hackman ; edited by Paula Kay Montgomery. -- 2nd ed.
    xiv, 136 p. 22x28 cm.
    Rev. ed. of: Library media skills and the senior high school
English program. 1985.
    Includes bibliographical references and index.
    ISBN 1-56308-544-5 (softbound)
    1. Library orientation for high school students--United States.
2. High school libraries--Activity programs--United States.
3. English language--Study and teaching (Secondary)--United States.
4. Library orientation for high school students--Maryland. 5. High
school libraries--Activity programs--Maryland. 6. English language--
Study and teaching (Secondary)--Maryland.  I. Montgomery, Paula
Kay.  II. Hackman, Mary H., 1931-    Library media skills and the
senior high school English program.  III. Title.
Z711.2.H29  1999
025.5'678223--dc21                                        98-53626
                                                               CIP

*This book is dedicated to my students*
*Past, present, and future.*
*Each of you gives me great hope for*
*The twenty-first century.*

*In honor of*
*A. Brian Helm*
*1947–1998*
*for the élan and vision*
*he brought to our profession*

# Contents

# Foreword

What constitutes mastery of information skills for high school students? By the time students reach grades 10 through 12, it is to be hoped that they have achieved competence in basic information seeking skills. The question for the library media specialist is which skills have been mastered at what level. In many cases, the students are now ready for refinement of those skills within the context of school assignments.

Information skills mastery is dependent upon the opportunity to use print and non-print resources. Multiple opportunities in all content areas must be provided and encouraged. Library and information skills should be practiced daily so that these skills are automatic. The question then becomes how are they incorporated into the routine and what constitutes the most adequate level of use.

In high school, it should be difficult to separate the library media center from the daily routine of classroom study. Resources contribute more to coursework than ever before. The library media specialist who is both aware of and active in curriculum development will be a partner with teachers to integrate necessary skills refinement into lessons and units of instruction. The primary places for integration of skills are the English-language arts and the social studies programs. Students read and study literature and produce information for others in the form of reports, papers, video productions, and Internet Web pages. Information skills processes taught in English and in social studies may form a stronger basis for the use of libraries throughout the rest of students' lives. The library media specialist and teachers have much in common. They work on the same goals, objectives, and lessons. As the library media specialist helps students find meaning through resources, the classroom teacher helps students find meaning in resources. Meaning is transmitted in the daily activities that students complete.

Mary Hackman has focused on the role of the library media specialist in determining the new skills necessary for mastery and refinement. She explores the relationships between library media specialists and teachers that help students use information and find meaning in resources. Discussions of how to publicize all services and how to create an environment where give and take occur are carefully presented through actual examples. Suggestions for interaction and for units of study are provided as models. The ideas in this book have been tested and have met with success.

The author, Mary H. Hackman, has been a high school library media specialist in Anne Arundel County Public Schools, Annapolis, Maryland. She served as the library media administrator for Baltimore County Public Schools before retiring. During her retirement from the school system, she served as the coordinator for the Graduate Library Media Program at Western Maryland College, Westminster, Maryland. As the coordinator for interns, she has had many opportunities to review instruction with new information sources. Her work with new library media specialists has convinced her of the importance of improved library media programs. Her wide experience has served new library media specialists well.

As readers examine the many examples and models presented in this book, they will see the change in emphasis in the use of information processes in a wide range of settings. The growth of the Internet as a source for learning and for finding information are reflected in the new skills frameworks. Chapters advance from a conceptual framework for how library and information skills might be integrated to the specifics of how the concepts have been put into practice. This revised work should benefit secondary library media specialists who wish to implement an active program in a high school.

Paula Kay Montgomery

# Preface

This book demonstrates ways in which the high school library media program and the English program can work together to integrate instruction. While each program stands on its own merits, when library information skills are taught in conjunction with subject area objectives, each program is stronger and, most important, more relevant to students. Several examples of integrated instruction and curriculum documents are provided in this book, and readers are encouraged to adapt these examples for their own use. Credit for the examples of curriculum models and lessons goes to English-language arts and library media personnel in the state of Maryland. Without a doubt, there are many other examples that could be used from Maryland, and I know from personal experience that exemplary programs also exist in the other states in this country. Maryland has made great strides in the use of information technology since the first edition of this book was published, and I have observed those advancements on many levels. There remains a distance to travel, however, and it seems there will always be new and better components to evaluate, learn, and teach or opportunities to examine what the neighboring school does and adapt it for one's own situation. That, basically, is the idea for this book. Here are some ideas tried in Maryland, based upon national goals, state standards, and local resources. The reader is invited to explore them.

# Acknowledgments

There are a number of special people to be acknowledged for the contents of this book. Those who are in the field of education will be listed by the Maryland school system in which they serve.

### Anne Arundel County Public Schools
- A. Brian Helm, Director, Library Media Services

### Baltimore County Public Schools
- Henry McGraw, Supervisor, English/Language Arts
- Della Curtis, Coordinator, Library Information Services
- Doris Glotzbach, Supervisor, Library Information Services
- Carolyn Mollenkopf, Professional Research Librarian
- Ann B. O'Neill, Library Media Specialist, Franklin Senior High School
- Carrie Everhart, Library Media Specialist, Catonsville Senior High School
- Kay Sullivan, Secretary, Library Information Services

### Carroll County Public Schools
- Irene Hildebrandt, Supervisor, Library Media Services
- Christian Conklin, English Teacher, Francis Scott Key High School
- Penny Foster, Library Media Specialist, Francis Scott Key High School
- Richard Salkin, English Teacher, Francis Scott Key High School
- Iris Wingert, Library Media Specialist, South Carroll High School

### Frederick County Public Schools
- Rebecca Reickel, English Teacher, Walkersville High School
- Kay Craig, Media Specialist, Walkersville High School

### Howard County Public Schools
- Allan Starkey, Coordinator, English/Language Arts

## Maryland State Department of Education
- Gail Bailey, Branch Chief, Office of School Library Media Services
- Gertrude Collier, Branch Chief, Office of Language Development and Early Learning

## Washington County Public Schools
- Roseann Fisher, Supervisor, Library Media Services

In addition to the people named above, thanks to those many individuals who worked on the various documents from each of the school districts. You are extraordinary professionals and deserve so much credit for the work you do.

Many thanks go to Paula Montgomery, who has made countless contributions to Maryland's school library media programs as former Chief of School Library Media Services Branch at the Maryland State Department of Education. More importantly, her influence is felt far beyond Maryland with her work as a consultant, the editor of *School Library Media Activities Monthly*, and, of course, as my editor and friend.

Speaking of editors, I owe a debt of gratitude to the editors at Libraries Unlimited, especially to Kay Mariea whose guidance has been most valuable and helpful.

Thanks also to my son-in-law, Michael Cantrell, who patiently guided me through the intricacies of the computer's word processing program and gave so generously of his time and expertise. And, I am indebted to my daughter Laura Hackman, who translated the word processing program into Microsoft Word in order for the publisher to read it. How does one thank a husband for putting up with the hours spent working on a book? James P. Hackman gets the "husband-of-the-year" award for understanding and patience.

# Chapter 1

## The Senior High School Library Media Specialist

As the dual forces of technological advancement and educational reform permeate the nation's schools, the library media specialist has both a special opportunity and an awesome task. Theoretically and realistically, every student who enters high school will come into contact with the library media specialist. And every student will come away from high school with an impression of the library media center and the people in it. As surely as every student leaves with an impression of the library media program, every teacher comes to the high school with an impression made from past experiences of what to expect from the library media specialist. When those past experiences were positive, the teachers ensure that their students make appropriate and creative use of the library media center. However, those teachers who have had negative contacts with library media personnel in previous assignments need to be reoriented to recognize the unlimited possibilities that await their students in the media center.

## Responsibilities of the Library Media Specialist

The library media specialist must be knowledgeable about every course taught in the high school, familiar with every member of the faculty and administrative staff, and a viable part of the school community as a whole. It is equally important that the school staff understand the large budgetary commitment required to operate a high school library media center. In addition to personnel, the budget provides for an inventory of print and non-print media; equipment to be supplied to every department in the school; facilities for darkrooms, television production, sound studios, computer laboratories, and storage to house innumerable supplies.

While it may be a simple matter to see the physical aspects of the center, there are many facets of the library media specialist's assignment that may not be readily apparent. The library media specialist is responsible for selecting, ordering, receiving, recording, cataloging, labeling, filing, placing, organizing, circulating, retrieving, inventorying, maintaining, discarding, and replacing all of the materials and equipment for which the media center is held responsible.

In addition, even the most elaborate and technologically current library media center is merely a repository if the specialist is not an active member of the school's instructional staff. In order to integrate library and information skills into the curriculum, the library media specialist must take into account all materials and equipment, all knowledge of course curricula, the varied interests of teachers and students, and all of

the skills he or she possesses to assist students in the process of learning. The library media specialist is a teacher with insight into the entire curriculum offered in the school. An awesome task indeed! All too often, under the pressure of the many duties to be performed, and in spite of the good intention of teaching high school students to be lifelong independent users of libraries, the library media specialist still points in the general direction of the center's catalog when a question is asked. If the student has no idea where to begin to search for an answer to a question, frustration will quickly result, and a negative image of libraries in general may be the outcome. If, however, the library media specialist teaches the student the process for finding answers to questions, whether it be through the catalog or the Internet, the student may need only a few verbal reminders to lead him or her in the correct direction. Certainly the student will have a more positive image of libraries upon which to build. How well does the library media specialist succeed in leading students to find the right answers? How much of the teaching done in the high school library media program carries over into life after high school?

 ## Effectiveness of Teaching Library and Information Skills

In 1979 a librarian from the University of Evansville in Illinois wrote in the *School Library Journal*:

> After two years of administering a very active undergraduate program, I find that incoming freshman—without a single exception that I have observed—lack all but the most rudimentary library skills. Not only are they unable to use reference tools, they have no inkling of what sources are available. They don't know when to ask questions or even what to ask for; they do not know whether a librarian has served them badly or well. For them, the unbounded universe of information is, literally, a closed book (Biggs 1979, 44).

Considerable evidence indicates there has been little change in the skills the college freshman brings into the college library. An informal survey of college and university librarians in Maryland I have conducted suggests that freshmen can use the computer for e-mail and to locate chat rooms, but they have difficulty in selecting the correct key words or making the necessary links to find relevant information for the task at hand. Usually college students are able to use the electronic catalog to determine the holdings of the library, but are unable to decide which resource would be of most value to solve their problem or answer their question. Evaluating the information (assuming it is located) is one of the more important lessons to be taught at the high school level. It stands to reason that if the college-bound student is not getting the necessary skills to locate, evaluate, and use information, neither are other students. The world also needs plumbers and auto mechanics and carpenters and clerical personnel who can read directions and analyze and interpret the information needed to accomplish their jobs. There will certainly be times when the ability to use key words will help these individuals access the information they need via the computer or a library's automated catalog. It is the responsibility of the school library media specialist, working in concert with the teacher, to provide students with the necessary skills.

What else can be done? Most districts have library and information skills as part of their instructional program. Library media specialists across the nation have developed a logical scope and sequence for teaching those skills in our school systems. The development of a scope and sequence of library media and information skills gives the library media specialist a primary responsibility in the instructional program; no longer can the specialist function in just a supportive role.

If one were to examine instructional program documents for library and information skills from school districts around the United States, one would find that those skills with which college freshmen come equipped are usually introduced in the elementary grades. The pattern for library media skills instruction at the elementary level is frequently one where classes are scheduled to go to the media center for a specified period of time on a regular basis. Part of that time is used for formal instruction and practice; the remainder of the time is used for browsing and book selection. Ideally, small groups and individual students may visit the library at any time for reference work, computer-based projects, or other library media skills-related activities. Many schools prefer that the times when the elementary students come to the library media center be flexibly scheduled to allow for better integration of skills instruction into the regular classroom work. The important thing is that every student in the elementary school gets library media instruction on a regular basis, whether that time is fixed or flexible.

The library media specialist in the elementary school works with fewer teachers than the specialist at the secondary level and could accomplish more with the integration of instruction, thereby making the skills taught more meaningful to the students. Since there are also fewer students at the elementary level than in high school, the library media specialist can more readily address the needs of the individual child. This does not imply that the elementary library media specialist has an easy job; on the contrary, it is a demanding job that requires huge amounts of time and energy. But look at the rewards! What is taught in the elementary school library media center gets reinforced again and again in secondary school and lasts a lifetime.

In my experience, the elementary student is exposed to a wide variety of books and is encouraged to read for pleasure (as well as practice) at every turn. *Information Power* stresses reading for pleasure as a vital motivational role of the library media specialist (AASL and AECT 1988). State standards for school library media programs consistently emphasize reading for pleasure and information as one of the most important factors in the profession. The opportunity to influence students to make this crucial choice is very prevalent in the primary and intermediate grades. How often does the high school teacher bring his or her class to the high school media center to choose a book to read for fun? Not very often, if at all. In high school, there is usually a bibliography from which to choose, a report of some variety to follow the reading, or an assigned project to dictate what is read. There are always those who are going to read for the pure pleasure of it, no matter how full their days may be, and in these cases, the school media specialist gets the opportunity to offer reading guidance to the science fiction fan, the mystery buff, or the historical fiction enthusiast. Usually, then, the high school student is using the media center to locate information and to utilize that information for a specific purpose. As the curriculum becomes more complex in the upper grades, it is obvious that the student must become more intent upon using the media center for information gathering. The library media specialist in the high school has the responsibility to teach those skills involved in locating, evaluating, and synthesizing that information and to continue to build upon those skills learned at previous levels.

What are the road blocks that cause the breakdown in the process of teaching library and information skills in an integrated program at the senior high school level? In the first place, it is impossible to schedule every student on a regular basis into the media center. Sheer numbers and the lack of space, personnel, and time make that a given. In the second place, teachers are hard pressed to get through all of the course content they are required to cover with their classes. In addition to classwork, there are standardized tests to be administered and specified subject matter to be taught prior to test day. Then there are assignments and mid-term and final examinations to be developed, administered, graded, and averaged in with other grades earned during that marking period.

Public education and the professionals engaged in it have become targets to be blamed for many of society's ills, and since high school is the final step in public education for many students, the high school educator bears the pressure of much of the criticism leveled at education today. Out of this criticism came essential curriculum, site-based management, the push for national standards in almost every subject area, an increased demand for excellence in the schoolhouse, and an overwhelmingly significant infusion of technology—all of which impact the high school instructional program. Another important factor has been the shift to block scheduling, or the four period day, in many high schools. While both negative and positive opinions are held with regard to this form of scheduling, it is one more adjustment for the high school instructional staff to make. It seems that change is the order of the day.

Another impediment to the integration of library and information skills into the curriculum is that most teachers do not have a background in school library media programs themselves and do not see the necessity for spending precious class time in the media center. (It has only been in the last two decades that our colleges and universities have made a concerted effort to teach bibliographic skills. Library instruction is not required by most of our institutions of higher learning—not even for those students who plan to become teachers.)

The final contributing piece to this dilemma has to be time, or the lack thereof. The teacher usually has one planning period each day, but that does not necessarily coincide with the time the library media specialist can meet with the teacher. The very process of sitting down to plan for integrated instruction is time consuming. In reality, planning together often occurs when the teacher comes to the library media center to ask when a particular class can be scheduled for a specific reason. Also, the teacher is a member of a subject area department within the school and attends regularly scheduled department meetings. Library media specialists who attend those meetings find them to be fertile ground for communication and can use those meetings to promote integrated skills instruction. However, the various departments in many senior high schools meet at the same time, and the library media specialist cannot be present at all of them.

It is common practice for department chairpersons to meet together on a regular schedule with the school administration; sometimes this group is called the school leadership team, the site-based management advisory council, or simply the administrative team. If the library media specialist is considered to be a department chairperson, this is a golden opportunity to find out what is happening in every department and begin work toward the process of integrating instruction. The problem with total dependence upon these sessions is that the library media specialist is going through an intermediary ( the department chairperson ) to get the message across to other teachers in the department. Department chairpersons have many responsibilities in addition to their teaching load, and there are many matters of business to discuss other than library and information skills integration.

There is one other factor that is crucial in any discussion about high school graduates who are lacking in library and information skills. Even though the numbers seem to be decreasing, there are still those media specialists—particularly at the high school level—who do not see themselves as teachers. There are those who were once teachers and looked to the media center as a way out of the classroom; some of these individuals readily admit that they did so to avoid the drudgery of correcting papers, keeping grade books, and handling the same discipline problems day after day. They are not interested in encouraging any kind of instruction, much less actively pursuing the process of integrated skills instruction. Other library media specialists graduated from colleges and universities with degrees that did not require any coursework in learning theory or instructional techniques. Library media centers operated by such individuals may offer excellent support services to the instructional programs in the school, but to fully integrate library and information skills into the curriculum, the library media specialist must accept the responsibility for teaching those skills. Other teachers in the school need to see the media specialist as a good teacher to whom they are willing to turn over pieces of their curriculum in order to provide students with the best learning environment possible. Unless these conditions are met, high school students will continue to enter college or the work force ill-prepared to use a library efficiently or to access necessary information.

 ## Integrating Library and Information Skills with Subject Area Skills

Programs have addressed the need for a vigorous plan to integrate library and information skills into all facets of the curriculum. These programs occur within a district when there is clear direction from the library media supervisor. They occur when the supervisor and other subject area supervisors look together at goals and outcomes to see how curriculum can accommodate the needs of the students in both the library media program and the particular subject matter. The attitude of the supervisor permeates the school setting and provides the climate and the support for the library media specialist to function more efficiently. When criteria has been clearly defined for both the classroom teacher and the library media specialist, the task of integrated skills teaching is facilitated.

The term *integrated instruction* has been used many times in this chapter. What is meant by integrated instruction? How does this differ from instruction that takes place in many library media centers? Thomas Walker and Paula Montgomery address these questions in their book, *Teaching Media Skills: An Instructional Program for Elementary and Middle School Students.*

Media specialists, in the past, have sought to "relate" media skills instruction to everyday classroom teaching rather than integrate the two. Teachers, on the other hand, have been perfectly willing for media specialists to "relate" media skills to classroom studies but have not, typically, integrated media skills objectives, activities, and assessments into instruction. The difference between the terms "relate" and "integrate" seems subtle at first, but the operational difference is enormous. Relating media skills to classroom instruction implies one set of instructional objects and a separate set of media skills objectives, one set of instructional activities and a separate set of media skills activities, one set of instructional assessments and a separate set of media skills assessments, all more or less related but, at the same time all very separate. Integrating media skills into classroom instruction, on the other hand, implies only one set of instructional objectives, activities, and assessments. An integrated approach to media skills instruction takes advantage of the strength and preparation of the teacher in instructional theory and methodology and the strength of the media specialist in the theory and application of instructional media. Instructional planning for media skills then emerges as a process of logically and equitably dividing labor between teacher and media specialist (Walker and Montgomery 1977, 13–14 ).

Where does one begin the process of putting together instructional objectives or outcomes, activities, and assessments and drawing upon the separate strengths of the classroom teacher and the media specialist? The senior high school has a multitude of courses to offer its students; some are required for graduation and others may be elected by the student for the sake of interest or vocational aptitude. The required courses that comprise the English curriculum have a natural affinity with library media skills. In the elementary school, reading is taught by the classroom teacher and fostered by the media specialist; the children are introduced to a wealth of children's books, magazines, videotapes and computer programs. The elementary school student develops the habit of coming to the media center to write reports and do projects. These kinds of activities involve aspects of the language arts or English program. At the senior high school level, every student is required to take English, usually every year. When the high school student is taken to the library media center for orientation in his or her freshman year, it is most often with the English class. As a rule, it is in the English class where the student learns the intricacies involved in writing a paper or developing a project, which may well include production techniques. If one were to ask the senior high school media specialist which department in the school makes the most use of the materials and facilities in the center, the answer would very often be the English department. It would seem logical, then, to begin the process of integrating objectives or outcomes, activities, and assessments with library information skills and the English curriculum. There are many pieces in this process and there are a variety of ways to proceed. In the following pages, we will examine some of the factors involved in this process and look at some proven plans of action.

# Chapter 2

## The English Teacher and the Librarian

In order to bring about change, it is extremely important to have a perspective of the past. As the English teacher and the media specialist consider the task of integrating library and information skills with the English curriculum, a brief look at both programs over the last few decades can assist in providing a rationale to continue to foster the communication that brings about change.

 ## Before the Sixties Revolution

Education is no different from other fields of endeavor in that if one is around long enough, one sees the pendulum swing from one extreme to the other and back again. The English classroom is representative of such changes, despite new technologies and new approaches to learning styles and instructional methodology. Prior to the "student revolution" in the 1960s, English was offered in the high schools strictly by grade level—English 9, English 10, English 11, and English 12. Often, too, the student was placed in a specific track and there he or she stayed. One either took the academic (or college-bound) course of study or one could choose from the commercial, vocational, or general courses. The only time a student was allowed to deviate from the "track" was to take a semester course in typing, home economics, or a practical shop course.

Sometimes classes were homogeneous; more often than not they were heterogeneous. Class sizes were always large, and English teachers considered themselves blessed if there were under thirty-five students in a class. Negotiated agreements were vagaries in the distant future and planning time was often usurped by assigned duties, extracurricular assignments, or that bane of the high school teacher's existence—study hall. The teacher followed a prescribed course of study for the year. If there were no district- or school-approved curricula, the textbook and suggested activities were used. With a course of study, English was divided into units lasting from four to eight weeks encompassing composition, grammar, literature, and speech, and was sometimes thematic in approach. As a rule, students were required to read at least one library book each marking period and prepare a written or oral report on that book. Lists of recommended books were the exception rather than the rule. This required reading was done outside of the classroom and in addition to a selection of classic literature that was prescribed for each grade level. It was not uncommon for the English teacher in the fifties to have between one hundred seventy-five and two hundred students in a day, and the task of keeping up with the ensuing paperwork was enormous. There was little time for reading guidance, and students were usually on their own when it came to book selection.

Literature was frequently approached as a survey course and was often correlated with the social studies program. If a tenth grade student was taking World History, then that same student was also taking a world literature survey course in the English class; if United States History was taught in the eleventh grade, a survey of American literature was the requirement for the English class. While there was no real effort to make the instruction exactly parallel, and no organized planning time allotted for the social studies teachers and the English teachers to work together, there was some correlation, and the student did have the opportunity to grasp the broader view of the time about which he or she was studying.

The high school library was used as the source for the ubiquitous book reports and for occasional reference work. Writing a term paper was a requirement in the twelfth grade academic English class as a general rule, and that endeavor took students to the high school library. It was the exception for the librarian in the high school to do any formal teaching. Instead, individual students were assisted in locating information for the term paper, and the breadth of information available in the reference section was seldom introduced.

I was a high school English teacher during the fifties and do not remember ever sending students to the high school library, much less taking them there. Instead, elaborate field trips were planned for twelfth grade English classes to visit the Enoch Pratt Free Library in Baltimore, located about twenty-five miles from that then relatively rural high school. At the Pratt, students were enthralled with the magnificence of the architecture, awed by the pervasive spirits that inhabited the Edgar Allan Poe Room, and overwhelmed by the wide variety of books introduced to them by the capable librarians of that prestigious institution. At the time, Pratt used its own system of cataloging and classification, one that was uniquely Pratt's. Undoubtedly, the students were justifiably confused by the disparities between the Dewey decimal system used at school and Pratt's system. One can only hope that the students understood that libraries need to have a system for organizing materials, whatever that system might be. Many of those same students returned to the high school following their graduation to relate how they had traveled from their college campuses to use the Pratt's collection for research work. Considering the breadth and depth of Pratt's collection at the time, those students were fortunate to have been introduced to one of the nation's finest public libraries. On the other hand, how unfortunate that those same students did not have equal opportunity to know that their high school had a certificated librarian and a small, but more than adequate, collection.

# The Sixties

Until 1957 and the advent of Russia's *Sputnik*, parents and other interested citizens had confidence in the public school system. Egon Guba tells us that the American people then began to wonder whether the deficiencies in science and technology could be traced to the process of education in the United States (Brickell 1975). In addition to *Sputnik, Brown v. the Board of Education* in 1956 and the resulting mandate for integration by the federal courts in 1958 placed additional demands upon our schools, affecting both the English curriculum and our libraries. Guba states that in the attempt to assuage the public outcry and solve the perceived problems in our schools, educators promised too much. In turn, public expectations were too high, and confidence in public education was further eroded.

 # New Methods and Courses

The upheaval of the sixties brought about changes in the colleges and universities; students began to demand a say in course content and structure. The senior high schools, yielding to public pressure to improve the quality of education and responding to the changes occurring in our institutions of higher learning, altered their course. Evidence quickly pointed to the fact that our schools were not adequately teaching the nation's poor and the minority groups. Educators tried instructional television, programmed learning, team teaching, and flexible scheduling—to name but a handful of the techniques tried in the sixties—but the quality of learning that ensued produced uneven results. The survey courses in American literature and British literature, once the bulwarks of the English curriculum and the textbook publishers, became things of the past. There were demands for the rights of students with special needs, for courses to be tailored for specific ethnic and racial groups, and for courses that were relevant to the rapidly changing world in which we found ourselves.

The English curriculum followed the pattern set by all subject areas as more and more courses became semesterized at the high school level. The resulting variety of high school courses became known as the "smorgasbord curriculum." Indeed, there was something for everyone; the principal problem for the student was what to take and when to take it. English classes were offered in film study, individualized reading, creative writing, theatre arts, specific authors, and specific literary genres. To add to the confusion, courses were given titles such as Fact and Fantasy, The American Dream, and English Patterns. One had to read course descriptions carefully in order to discern exactly what was being offered. Previously, Ms. Smith and Mr. Jones had always taught eleventh grade English, now every member of the department taught semester-length classes in what was often an ungraded classroom. While the number of students taught by the English teacher decreased, the number of preparations increased significantly. Teachers and guidance counselors alike became advisors to help students at every grade level sort through the myriad choices, not just in English, but through the entire curriculum.

The ungraded classroom was an attempt to allow the high school student even greater freedom of choice and to take responsibility for his or her own learning. Sometimes there were clear prerequisites, but not always. The sophomore could no longer assume it was proper to take World Literature in the tenth grade because his or her senior sibling could be enrolled in the same class. The security of knowing that as a student you would be competing with members of your own grade was gone. The more adept students were encouraged to reach higher and work harder, and the less adept were often surprised that they could do as well as some of the upper classmen. Needless to say, all students were not so fortunate.

 ## Changes in the School Library

During the sixties, school libraries became the focus of national attention primarily because funding had been negligible, and with the emphasis placed on the sciences and the dramatic increase in course offerings, it became evident that districts could not handle the additional expense to augment school library acquisitions—acquisitions that would support the new curriculum. In 1965 the federal government passed the Elementary and Secondary Education Act (ESEA), which afforded school libraries the money and the opportunity to purchase needed materials. Initially, there was little from which to choose. Publishers were as unprepared for this bonanza as were the school librarians. Multiple copies of often mediocre titles became the fare to stimulate the student to higher and loftier pursuits. But school librarians coped as best they could with purchases that had to be made within a short period of time and with more paperwork than one could imagine. Those school libraries that acquired the most creditable collections during the ESEA years were those where the librarian consulted with teachers who were teaching new courses and sought their advice prior to purchase. The subject area teacher received on-site assurance of material that supported the curriculum and was included in the decision of what to buy for perhaps the first time in his or her career.

In 1969 a new set of standards for librarians was published. *Standards for School Library Media Programs* was written as a joint effort by the American Association of School Librarians (AASL) and the National Education Association's Department of Audiovisual Instruction (DAVI). The terms *media specialist* and *media program* proliferated this document. The 1969 standards did not advocate actually changing the titles of librarian and library, but the forecast was there. The emphasis of those standards was on the vital role of the media center (AASL and DAVI 1969). Things were changing; the librarian, like the rest of the educators, was going to have to run to catch up.

More interaction continued to be required between the librarian and the other staff members. As courses were being rewritten and as teachers were required to teach more courses, input from the teachers was essential to keep the collection current with the curriculum. It was impossible to rely on the old, standard classics when the purpose of literature classes in the English program was to deal with the world today and to address current thinking. There had to be interaction with the librarian if there were to be supplemental reading assignments and, in some cases, any reading assignments at all. The randomly selected titles for the book reports of the last decade were replaced with specific titles aimed at enabling greater understanding of the classroom assignment. In many instances the librarian became an active part of the teaching team and indeed was expected to teach. Interestingly enough, there were those librarians who refused to accept the fact that audiovisual materials were authentic additions to their library collections, and audiovisual equipment was strictly off limits.

Resistance to change permeated the ranks of the librarians themselves. Some states and districts were fortunate to have leadership from strong, yet sympathetic library supervisors who provided assistance with in service courses and individual guidance and who never wavered from facilitating the changes they knew were to be a part of the profession for many years to come.

 ## The Seventies and Eighties

In 1975 a new set of standards for the school librarian was published. This time the Association for Educational Communications and Technology (formerly the National Education's Department of Audiovisual Instruction) worked with the American Association of School Librarians and produced *Media Programs: District and School*. While these standards were quantitative with regard to collections and numbers of pieces of equipment, the librarian would become the library media specialist. Around the country, state departments of education would respond by changing existing state requirements for the school librarian. There was reference to program objectives, and the library media specialist emerged as teacher. Concurrently, new technologies assumed a greater role in the schools, and the library media specialist had responsibility for equipment. Distribution, simple maintenance, and inventory became the province of the school's library media program. The media specialist was responsible for training all faculty and staff in the operation and use of each piece of equipment. Students were trained as audiovisual helpers and distributed equipment according to a faculty sign-up sheet kept in the AV room. They also served as troubleshooters when equipment failed to operate properly. Also, the media specialist was expected to teach students how to use production equipment to create slide tape programs and overhead transparencies to accompany various classroom assignments. Some schools assigned a willing teacher to the audiovisual portion of the job and gave the teacher an extra planning period plus a stipend in return for services rendered.

By the mid- to late-seventies, industrial and business leaders joined the colleges and universities in telling the senior high schools that students were graduating from their institutions who were unable to do the job or pass the course because they lacked even basic skills. Colleges were spending valuable time and money on remedial courses, and the public in general was unhappy with the state of our schools. High schools took the brunt of the criticism primarily because of declining Student Aptitude Test (SAT) scores. High school programs were failing at the job of preparing students to enter the world as effective, knowledgeable citizens. "Back to basics" was the catchphrase heard again and again in faculty rooms, college classrooms, boardrooms, and, of course, in the news media. High schools began to pare away at their curriculum. Where previously it was not uncommon to offer students as many as forty or fifty English courses, offerings were cut in half; again there were specific requirements, and prerequisites returned to the scene. As SAT scores began to edge upward again in the early eighties, there was renewed interest in the English program. Many states required students to pass proficiency examinations in order to receive their diplomas. Two of these examinations affected the English program: reading and writing. Once again the English program was revised, and the tried and true classics returned to the classroom. The English teacher and the library media specialist had difficulty convincing the publishers that it was time to return to new issues of old titles.

ESEA money was gradually being taken from the school library media center and used at the discretion of district administrators. It became more and more difficult to get the funding for media centers to keep current with curriculum changes and advancing technologies. Time was spent (especially by supervisors) in trying to convince boards of education of the importance of keeping collections up-to-date. Students, parents, and school-based personnel often joined in the public relations effort, and there were small successes in some school districts.

In 1988, *Information Power: Guidelines for School Library Media Programs* was published by a joint committee from the American Association of School Librarians and the Association for Educational Communications and Technology.

This new set of guidelines targeted the building-level library media specialist, emphasizing the need to create partnerships with the school administration and faculty to develop a library media program that would meet the specific requirements of the school curriculum. The roles of the library media specialist are defined as three-fold: information specialist, teacher, and instructional consultant. The last two roles were familiar to the library media specialist, but information specialist was a new term used to describe the reality of the job. As computers, databases, CD-ROMs, and interactive distance learning make their way into the library media program, the dire necessity to combine those roles becomes crucial as the media program seeks to help the learner find his or her way through the maze of available information.

 ## The Nineties

Many of the challenges whose roots lie earlier in the twentieth century managed to come to the forefront in the nineties decade. The high schools are awash with change: there is the four-period day; the magnet school; violence among teens, which has spilled over from the inner city into suburbia; teen pregnancy; increased immigration; AIDS; the proliferation of drugs; advocacy for school choice; site-based management; and newer and faster technology, particularly the Internet. The millennium is upon us, ready or not, and setting the priorities regarding services, purchases, personnel, publicity, technologies, and instruction has to be a careful and thoughtful process for the school library media specialist. It cannot be accomplished in isolation. The need to work closely with teachers and administrative staff is more crucial than ever.

One of the changes brought about by the rapid growth in technology has been the diversion of funds. Library media budgets were usually limited to media and supplies; now the media specialist is being permitted to use the print and non-print budget to purchase equipment, specifically computers, or upgrades for existing computers. With the ability to use the computer to

access information through the Internet, the change in budget policy was not a difficult decision for district administrators and boards of education to make. This change, too, presents the library media specialist (a.k.a. information specialist) with a dilemma and the need to keep in close touch with teacher colleagues. What print purchases are necessary to support newly written curriculum? How many computers are needed in the library media center to satisfy the needs of the instructional program? Decisions and more decisions to make and, sometimes with very little guidance.

The impact of the four-period day upon both the library media program and the English program has been interesting. The English teacher is able to get through more material in ninety minutes than he or she could in two fifty-minute periods, and teaching styles have had to change. There is more group work; there is more interest when the student can complete the reading of a short story, discuss its characterization, plot, and relationship to present-day life, as well as complete an activity with peers relating to that story. When the English teacher brings the class to the media center to do research on the author of the story for a critical essay, there is time to locate the necessary information from several sources—print and non-print and Web pages—evaluate that information, and write the essay. And perhaps, the time can be found to return those materials to be easily located by the next class! In the past, students would complain as the class period ended: "But I just got started!" Now, with clear direction from the library media specialist, the task can often be completed in one sitting. There are those teachers who dislike the longer periods—though there are few complaints about a ninety-minute planning period—and have had a difficult time adjusting to this change. Generally, informal conversations with teachers and media specialists, as well as students, lead me to believe that the four-period day is successful.

In the nineties, the card catalog is almost gone, having been taken over by automated catalog systems. There is not as much time given over to the cataloging of books and non-print media or the seemingly endless task of typing cards for all media. The job of inventory has been simplified by the bar code and the computer's wand. But somehow, the job does not get any easier. The same is true for the English teacher.

Baltimore's newspaper, *Baltimore Sun*, ran a series of three articles in 1997 about Centennial High School in Maryland's Howard County. This school has the justifiable reputation of being one of the best high schools in the nation, with SAT scores outperforming both state and national averages by better than 100 points. There are many reasons for this kind of performance, including well-educated parents with above-average incomes. One of the highest-level courses offered is Humanities 3, consisting of Advanced Placement History and Gifted and Talented English with art and music intertwined, and it is taught by an English teacher and a history teacher. This appears to be a thoroughly integrated course; when the history curriculum deals with the Great Depression, the students are reading *Grapes of Wrath*, listening to jazz, and creating stained glass windows to

fit the subject matter. These students have a seven-chapter, eighty-page minimum paper to produce during their course of study. In all probability there are many resources at their disposal, but when permitted to do so, these students would visit the Library of Congress for primary sources. The English teacher in this team, M. H. Lankin, retired in June 1997 after thirty years of teaching. Ms. Lankin estimates that she graded 1,430 essays during the 1996–97 school year taking anywhere from 15 minutes to 1-$\frac{1}{2}$ hours to read (*Baltimore Sun*, June 17, 1997). Her primary reason for retiring is the "immense pressure of work." One marvels at the kind of commitment required to have dedicated that kind of time and energy to students, but the rewards have to be satisfying. The library media center was not the focus of this series of articles, but I am familiar with the center, its personnel, and its program; one can be certain that the students from the Humanities 3 class were welcomed and appropriately assisted in the library media center as they sought to find information required for the class. The library media center at Centennial High School has more than adequate resources and the technology to access the world of information beyond its walls.

The demands placed on all educators today is extraordinary, and the demands have to be even greater in inner city schools that enroll large numbers of students from underprivileged homes who enter the classroom with feelings of hopelessness and antagonism, rather than enthusiasm and motivation. Each decade has had its challenges that have been met with varying degrees of success. Many of those challenges remain as schools try to adjust to a changing society.

It would seem that the bond between the English teacher and the media specialist will continue to grow as budgets focus on the technologies that provide information and less attention is paid to the quality of the information itself. By working together, one would expect that students would learn what questions to ask and how to assess the quality of the sources from which their answers are obtained.

# Chapter 3

## English and Library Information Skills— The Alignment

This book does not pretend to provide a study on the development of curriculum design or instructional development in either English or library media and information skills. However, this chapter will discuss some evaluation techniques and some approaches to curriculum development.

##  Curriculum Development

What, exactly, is curriculum? *Curriculum Design—Fundamental Curriculum Decisions* prepared by the Association of Supervision and Curriculum Development, 1983 Yearbook Committee and written by George Beauchamp, gives a variety of definitions for curriculum and curriculum design, but the most widely accepted definition of curriculum by educators is simply a course of study for the learner. Curriculum as we know it today reaches far beyond "course of study" and attempts to address many other far-reaching issues. George Beauchamp describes curriculum as "a written plan for the educational program of a school or schools. Curriculum design, then, will consist of those considerations having to do with the contents, the form, and the various elements of a curriculum. We distinguish between curriculum planning and instructional planning with the curriculum planning being the antecedent task" (Beauchamp 1983, 90). He also states, "Scope and sequence have long been two major problems in curriculum design. The display of course content into topical outline is one way planners can watch for discrepancies in scope and sequence. It also helps with horizontal articulation among the various subjects" (Beauchamp 1983, 97).

Curriculum documents usually begin with a statement of goals and objectives or outcomes. Keep in mind that much of the actual design is arbitrary and is left with the planners. Goals are usually followed by content: content being what will actually be taught. Specific activities are included, as well as a means of determining whether the intended learner reaches the specified goals. A list of possible resources is another component of most curriculum guides. One of the most important things to understand about curriculum design is that it is never finished; it is an ongoing process. When the curriculum is being revised, pieces of the original plan are often kept intact. If any curriculum is to be vital and continue to meet the ever-changing needs in a technological society, flexibility must be the key.

The decision to revise curriculum should never be preemptory; assessment of the need to revise is essential. When a district determines that the English curriculum needs to be rewritten, many factors have to be considered. The decision to revise is reached after considering such factors as the results of standardized test scores, follow-up studies of the district's graduates, changing college and job requirements, the resolve to phase in new technology, or the implementation of new district or school goals.

One way to develop or revise curriculum is through the work of a carefully selected committee. The English supervisor of the district and other professional personnel form a committee to create or revise the curriculum. The ideal committee should consist of the English supervisor, appropriate English teachers, at least one media specialist, an administrator, citizens from the community, and high school students. There is no set rule as to the makeup of the committee—except that it should be representative of those who will be affected by the revision. The committee will adjust goals and objectives to meet the needs indicated in the assessment; content will be tailored to the adjusted goals and objectives;

activities will be written to reflect the content; and resources will be chosen to reinforce the content. Methods of evaluation, an essential part of the curriculum guide, will determine how well the goals and objectives are met.

In the past, if a library media specialist was a member of the curriculum committee, his or her function was usually to determine whether the selected resources were in print. Sometimes that function would include finding new materials to be used in implementing the content and providing support for the suggested activities as they were written. These are certainly important functions—necessary functions. How many times has curriculum been written only to discover that some of the key resources listed were out of print and no longer available? Part of the function of any curriculum committee must be to check *Books in Print* (which is accessible in book or electronic format), current publishers' and producers' catalogs, and to acquire materials for review and evaluation by committee members prior to inclusion in a curriculum document.

The library media specialist serves as an instructional consultant on the committee formed to revise curriculum and has input into the goals and outcomes, the content, the activities, and the process of assessment, as well as the development of a current resource list. An accurate inventory of equipment owned by district schools should be considered, as CD-ROMs and Internet sites are included along with print and non-print resources. Often it is wise to encourage the individual school to look at available resources and then add or delete items, as appropriate, for that program in a specific school. The media specialist (and everyone else on the committee) should be selected carefully. He or she must be an outstanding teacher with a thorough working knowledge of the library media program of skills, as well as having considerable familiarity with the specific subject area involved. Again, the library media specialist should remember that other committee members come to the planning sessions with a perspective of library media personnel that is based upon their previous experiences. There are many teachers in a school and many more teachers in the experience of a lifetime, but one can usually count the number of school library media professionals encountered on one hand. If some of those encounters with media personnel have been negative, there will be reluctance to turn over an important part of the curriculum design to someone about whom the committee member has concerns. Sometimes it becomes necessary for the specialist to do some re-educating on the spot and to solicit the aid of the committee chairperson to reinforce the value of having library media personnel involved in the important task of curriculum development.

When an objective or outcome is selected for inclusion in the revised curriculum guide, the media specialist should examine it carefully for a possible match with the library and information skills document. Can library and information skills be a part of the content? Can an activity be developed that will implement the content by using the library media center? How can the library media specialist assist in the assessment of specific objectives? What resources are available that will most advantageously address the needs of the content and help fulfill the stated outcomes? This does not mean that the media specialist spends quantities of valuable committee time propagating the library media program; the concentration must be on the subject area curriculum. But when there is an obvious match with the two programs, it should be examined and brought to the attention of the committee. This same information must be shared with all library media personnel in the district if there is to be a true alignment of library media skills and the subject involved.

The planning/writing stage of curriculum development is merely the first step in the delivery of instruction and, ultimately, learning. Curriculum is piloted and assessed prior to its use throughout a school or school system. The library media staff would logically have valuable contributions to make during these stages of curriculum development. The specialist in a school where new curriculum is being piloted may evaluate resources and determine a variety of ways in which library media services and the teacher could utilize those resources in facilitating learning. Teaching strategies and learning styles may be evaluated in order to determine what works best and for whom. In my experience, when library media personnel are judiciously selected and wisely used in curriculum design, those responsible for the process seek ways to include them in future efforts.

As new or revised curriculum is being implemented in a pilot program, it is essential for those associated with it to remember that the activities and resources are usually just suggested. There may be numerous ways to meet the desired goals and to deliver the content, and there may be resources on hand that could be used effectively. It is in the evaluative part of the curriculum design where one can truly determine how successful the plan actually is. Were the objectives or outcomes met? Did the students demonstrate learning through the various activities used in the classroom and the media center? Can the plan be adapted for a variety of student levels and individual needs? What resources could be added to make the plan as current as possible? What needs to be deleted?

The process of curriculum development or revision is an expensive proposition. Often summer workshops provide personnel and resources to write curriculum; this certainly means an impact upon the education budget. If curriculum is written during the school year, substitutes have to be hired to allow the personnel involved the time to work together. Time and money are at a premium in school systems, and it should be obvious that curriculum is not going to be revised every year or two. Including library media personnel in the planning, the writing, the piloting, the assessing, and revising of a program is cost-effective in determining the availability and applicability of resources and an additional budget source to be used to provide at least some of those resources. Time can be saved when the library media specialist interacts with subject area personnel during the planning and development of curriculum to determine the needs of the high school staff in the delivery of the curriculum. For example, the media specialist is the logical person to do staff development when there is a need to use Internet sites or use computer software with which the high school teacher may have little familiarity.

There may be activities that can be suggested where the media specialist can take the lead and introduce students to the information search process utilizing traditional and computer-driven resources. When the media specialist is involved from the very beginning, library and information skills become a natural part of the subject area curriculum.

If examining the development of a library and information skills program, one could expect to read about a committee formed consisting of media specialists, the supervisor, subject area teachers, administrators and students, as well as community members. As skills in information literacy are incorporated into the library media program, the example would show that it is extremely important to get a sense of the needs in other subject areas to properly align the scope and sequence. Since English and library and information skills are the two areas of concern in this book, how else can the integration of the two programs occur if curriculum does not address the duality?

 ## Program Evaluation

Once the program is developed and instructional planning occurs within the school, what are some ways to look at evaluating the effectiveness of the overall program? There are a variety of evaluation techniques used at the local or district level; these include observation in the classroom and media center by school-based administrators, central office supervisory staff, department chairpersons, and sometimes one's peers. While the primary purpose of these observations is usually to assess the teaching strategies used by the teacher or specialist, there is considerable emphasis placed upon instructional planning—a significant objective in curriculum development. The library media specialist is in a position of being evaluated each time a class comes to the media center. The classroom teacher usually remains with the class at the high school level, and it is not uncommon for the specialist to ask for feedback from the teacher. There are other forms of district or school level assessment based upon local testing programs, data collected from graduates, and even community reaction to specific programs in the school.

One form of evaluation at the senior high school level has been a constant, and that is the assessment completed every ten years through the auspices of the National Study of School Evaluation (NSSE) and its publication, *Evaluative Criteria for the Evaluation of Secondary Schools*. It should be noted that this publication will be used by many secondary schools through the year 2000, and certainly, it is the document with which most educators are familiar during the decade of the nineties. However, NSSE has published a new document, available in 1997 and 1998, titled *Indicators of Schools of Quality*, and this will be the tool used for evaluative purposes. The differences in the documents are addressed later in this chapter. Most high schools participate in this evaluative procedure because it leads to the accreditation of the school by the National Association of Colleges and Secondary Schools. Each school must examine the criteria and evaluate its own programs; the self-evaluation is done by a school-based committee whose composition is similar to a curriculum committee, consisting of the department chairperson of the subject area, several teachers from that department, other teachers, parents, an administrator, and students. Each program is judged on the basis of the goals and objectives formulated at the school level. Guidelines for the evaluative procedure also take into consideration the overall philosophy of the particular school.

Every high school English teacher and library media specialist who has been through the evaluation process has been exposed to *Evaluative Criteria* and has had the opportunity to examine the major expectations for each subject area. The sixth edition of *Evaluative Criteria* states the following expectations for the English program:

# The English Program

The English program is designed to improve students' awareness of the important role that language and literature play in their personal lives and career development. Essential to its overall program of studies, the English program emphasizes the development of oral and written comprehension, critical thinking skills and coherence, cogency and fluency in the expression and communication of ideas.

While the English program stresses competence in skills of reading, writing, speaking and listening, it also provides experiences and activities to help students become discriminating users of print and non-print media. Literary and media works, which are selected for both excellence in content and style and relevance to students' interests, will promote humanistic attitudes, aesthetic appreciation and critical evaluation skills while also providing models for leisure time activities.

The following are major expectations commonly associated with an effective English program.

- Students read, comprehend, interpret, evaluate and respond with an effective English program.
- Students read and respond to various genres of significant world literature.
- Students write as a means of developing fluency and as a tool for learning.
- Students write standard English in a grammatically acceptable, coherent and well organized manner.
- Students speak effectively in formal and informal situations to communicate ideas and information and to ask and answer questions.
- Students listen critically and analytically.
- Students develop critical thinking skills through the study and use of the English language and significant literature (NSSE 1987).

National Study of School Evaluation (NSSE). 1987. *Evaluative Criteria for the Evaluation of Secondary Schools*, 6th edition. Falls Church, Va: National Study of School Evaluation.

Part of *Evaluative Criteria* is labeled "Descriptive Criteria," and it is this section that represents what the self-assessment portion of the evaluation process recognizes as relevant to the specific subject area. This section consists of areas to evaluate: "Organization for Instruction," "Description of Offerings," and "Instruction." These sections list various strategies and desired outcomes that are graded 5,4,3,2,1, with 5 representing the highest achievement. The selected subject area committee, after reaching consensus, must give a rating to each criteria listed. Within the section for the English program, there are a number of these individual criteria that apply directly or indirectly to the library media program. For example:

- "Students are taught to use the media center and reference resources in relation to their needs.
- Students' leisure reading is promoted through projects such as paperback book stores, media center displays and literary clubs.
- A close liaison exists between English teachers and the public library.
- Adequate provisions are made for the use of computer software and hardware.
- Provision is made for the production of teacher- and student-made materials.
- Teachers consult regularly with media faculty about the acquisition and utilization of resources and services (NSSE 1987).

There can be little doubt that the educators who developed *Evaluative Criteria* saw a strong need for the English department to work with the school library media program. As a result, since 1987, there has been a national emphasis upon the alignment of the two programs. As NSSE publishes new and different assessment instruments, one would anticipate changes in format and emphasis, but one would also expect the bond between English and the library media program to have even greater significance.

To further augment the alignment of the two programs, the library media section of *Evaluative Criteria* (titled "Learning Media Services" in the sixth edition) states:

# Major Expectations

One of the important purposes of the educational program is to provide the student with a variety of self-enriching ideas and experiences which lead to intellectual curiosity, achievement and the establishment of a life-long pattern of learning. Utilization of human resources and the full range of media—which includes printed, audiovisual, computerized and other forms of information storage, retrieval and communication, as well as their accompanying technologies—are required to implement the purposes and programs of the school. The nationally recognized trend is to unify library, audiovisual, computer and other electronic services into a single administrative unit.

The following are major expectations commonly associated with an effective learning media program.

- Students recognize the importance of open information systems in contemporary society and actively seek differing points of view.
- Students make use of learning media resources and services.
- Students express themselves in a variety of media formats.
- Students bring critical judgments to bear upon the selection of appropriate resources to meet their needs and interests.
- Students use appropriate strategies, including the use of computerized data bases, in their search for information.
- Students express positive attitudes toward the use of the learning resource center.
- Students, faculty, administrators, parents and other members of the community are served by the learning media program (NSSE 1987, 453).

National Study of School Evaluation (NSSE). 1987. *Evaluative Criteria for the Evaluation of Secondary Schools*, 6th edition. Falls Church, Va: National Study of School Evaluation.

In the section dealing with the evaluation of the media program, the following descriptive criteria are but several examples from those listed for the in-school committee to assess.

The media program:

- Is an integral component of the total educational program.
- Provides for the coordination of the procurement, availability and utilization of materials.
- Observes the law dealing with the reproduction and utilization of copyrighted materials (NSSE 1987, 460).

Services to students:

- Provide for a comprehensive program of guidance in the developing of skills in reading, viewing and listening.
- Provide for the development of research and reference skills to achieve independence in learning.
- Assist students in the use of available networks of libraries and information centers.
- Include instruction in the searching of data bases (NSSE 1987, 460).

Services to faculty:

- Provide indexes and bibliographies of media to aid in selecting materials for instructional planning and use.
- Provide the development of resource lists on selected subjects.
- Provide professional assistance in the production of media.
- Provide assistance in the enrichment of course content and the design of instructional strategies (NSSE 1987, 460).

These descriptive criteria are merely samplings from a comprehensive document, but these examples make it clear that the school library media program should have an integrated program that affects every department in the school.

Following the self-examination process that is undertaken by the school, a committee from one of the geographical arms of the National Association of Colleges and Secondary Schools will visit and examine minutely the results of the school study and make its own observations. Members of the committee will talk with students, teachers, parents, and administrators and give a brief oral assessment prior to leaving the school. The visiting committee members will spend long hours working on a written draft of recommendations and commendations for each of the school's instructional programs and the overall school administration and climate. Eventually, the school will receive a written analysis of the work done by the in-school committees and the NSSE committees. It is important that the written report be shared with the entire staff and goals developed to work toward any recommendations that have been made.

As one looks at this whole formal evaluative process, which lasts about two years in preparation and delivery time (understanding, of course, that evaluation is an ongoing practice), there are many opportunities for other types of evaluation. Certainly, most important is the opportunity to examine one's own program, but one may also participate in the examination of other programs within the school or be open to an evaluation by an outside group of fellow educators. Central office administrators and supervisors need to be a significant part of this process to assist in implementing the necessary changes recommended and to see for themselves the quality of education in a specific school. This evaluative process requires that teachers, administrators, parents, and students work together and discover just what is expected from each discipline within the school. The opportunity for positive relationships to be formed is unique in the experience of the library media program and every other program as well. The library media specialist can certainly use this assessment process as a major factor in delineating his or her roles as teacher, information specialist, and instructional consultant. If, for whatever reason, the library media specialist is not delivering the kind of program detailed in *Evaluative Criteria*, it will be all too obvious and recommendations for improvement would be expected.

## NSSE's *Indicators of Schools of Quality*

In the late fall of 1997, the National Study of School Evaluation published an entirely new document to be used by the school for evaluation purposes. Volume 1 is titled *Indicators of Schools of Quality: Schoolwide Indicators of Quality*, and the foreword tells the reader that this change is the result of lengthy study and the need for a different approach to the school's individual evaluation and the onsite team visits. This document is research-based and is applicable to elementary, middle, and senior high schools, which is indeed a different approach from the former *Evaluative Criteria*. Another departure from the former criteria is the fact that this new document does not encourage any specific approaches for school improvement; instead, schools are asked to look for the best way to put the indicators of quality to work to address the individual needs of students in a particular educational setting. This publication consists of two volumes; the first deals with schoolwide indicators of quality, and Volume 2 addresses program-level indicators of quality. While Volume 2 will be the working document, used specifically by school programs to assess the level of quality achieved and to determine where improvements should be made, Volume 1 is comprehensive and gives the reader a taste of what is to come.

"An emphasis should be placed on clearly defining the essential knowledge and skills for student learning and then identifying meaningful, substantive connections across these goals for student learning that can provide students with an integrated and coherent instructional program" (NSSE 1997, 18). Six schoolwide goals have been identified by NSSE and the Alliance for Curriculum Reform. These goals and their performance indicators are shown on pages 24–25.

# Schoolwide Goals for Student Learning

**Learning-to-Learn Skills**

- Students make a commitment to creating quality work and striving for excellence.
- Students use a variety of learning strategies, personal skills, and time management skills to enhance learning.
- Students reflect on and evaluate their learning for the purpose of improvement.

**Expanding and Integrating Knowledge**

- Students connect knowledge and experiences from different subject areas.
- Students use what they already know to acquire new knowledge, develop new skills, and expand understanding.
- Students demonstrate integrated knowledge and skills in applying multidisciplinary approaches to solving problems or completing tasks.

**Communication Skills**

- Students communicate with clarity, purpose and understanding of audience.
- Students integrate the use of a variety of communication forms and use a wide range of communication skills.
- Students recognize, analyze and evaluate various forms of communication.

**Thinking and Reasoning Skills**

**Critical Thinking, Problem-Solving, and Creative Thinking**

- Students gather and use information effectively to gain new information and knowledge, classify and organize information, support inferences and justify conclusions appropriate to the context and audience.
- Students utilize, evaluate and refine the use of multiple strategies to solve a variety of types of problems.
- Students generate new and creative ideas by taking considered risks in a variety of contexts.

**Interpersonal Skills**

- Students work with others in a variety of situations to set and achieve goals.
- Students manage and evaluate their behavior as group members.
- Students deal with disagreement and conflict caused by diversity of opinions and beliefs.

**Personal and Social Responsibility**

- Students take responsibility for personal actions and act ethically (e.g., demonstrate honesty, fairness, integrity).

- Students respect themselves and others, and understand and appreciate the diversity and interdependence of all people.

- Students demonstrate an understanding of and responsibility for global and environmental issues.

- Students act as responsible citizens in the community, state and nation (NSSE 1997, 19).

National Study of School Evaluation (NSSE). 1997. *Indicators of Schools of Quality*. Vol. 1. Schaumburg, Ill.: National Study of School Evaluation.

---

In Part 1 of *Indicators of Schools of Quality*, each of the goals is delineated with examples of discipline-based Performance Indicators in a subject-by-subject and level-by-level format. English-language arts and library media services are prominent in the examples given. A rubric for evaluating the level of performance is given for each of the goals as well. Part 1 concludes with a sample report. Part 2 is labeled "Focusing on the Quality of the Work of the School" and includes quality instructional systems, quality organizational systems—part of which allows for input on the school's mission and goals—and provides an example of a report on the section. Part 3 is "Putting the Indicators of Schools of Quality to Work in Behalf of School Improvement." This section stresses the importance of not just looking at the status of the school as it stands today, rather the emphasis is on using *Indicators of Schools of Quality* as a tool to use to improve the conditions that improve student learning. It provides a series of questions, a format that can be used as a planning instrument for school improvement, and finally, an extensive list of resources that can be used by schools to further their understanding of

various aspects of the research available in education, as well as some models for implementing improvement plans.

This publication is worthy of close examination by everyone associated with schools as a guide in keeping with the tenor of the times. School improvement plans proliferate among educational institutions, with good reason, and this document can give valuable assistance, no matter the level of the school involved. It is particularly gratifying, for purposes of this book, to see that national leaders in the fields of English-language arts and school library media programs are included as contributing representatives to the content.

Until *Indicators of Schools of Quality* becomes widely used as the tool for high school assessment and improvement, *Evaluative Criteria* remains in place, and NSSE continues to support the underlying principles of that document. Obviously, both publications encourage and expect to see integration of library media programs with every other subject offered in the school. Assessment processes specifically designed to address library media programs will be examined in another chapter.

# Chapter 4

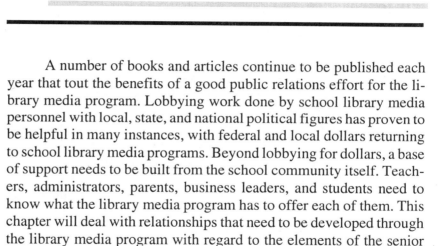

## Building Relationships

A number of books and articles continue to be published each year that tout the benefits of a good public relations effort for the library media program. Lobbying work done by school library media personnel with local, state, and national political figures has proven to be helpful in many instances, with federal and local dollars returning to school library media programs. Beyond lobbying for dollars, a base of support needs to be built from the school community itself. Teachers, administrators, parents, business leaders, and students need to know what the library media program has to offer each of them. This chapter will deal with relationships that need to be developed through the library media program with regard to the elements of the senior high school English curriculum.

 ## The Library Media Supervisor

Communicating effectively is probably the most important element in any public relations program. Previously in this book, I stated that the school library media specialist must have a good working relationship with every department in the senior high school; likewise, the library media supervisor must have a good relationship with every subject area supervisor and every department within the central administrative offices. The expression *working relationship* implies communication and the ability to work together successfully at a task. In a large school district, it is unlikely that the school-based library media personnel will acquire knowledge of the kinds of assistance available at the central office level other than from the library media supervisor and his or her staff. It is the responsibility of the library media supervisor to identify those teams of individuals within a school system who can be of assistance to the school-based personnel. For example, a centrally based team working with school personnel in a program for gifted and talented students in English may provide resource help to develop library and information skills activities designed for that particular group. Those who are responsible for inservice training with distance learning teachers may include the library media specialist to ensure there is understanding and support provided for the students involved. The English department would be interested in knowing about the word processing capabilities of the computer laboratory, as well as the variety of software available for the English student. What kinds of help are available when the English supervisor designates their high school to pilot a new curriculum? If the media specialist is not included in the planning stage, there could be few resources available in the school media center. It is vital that the library media supervisor know what is happening in the English program at the district level, identify sources of help for the school-based library media personnel, and communicate that information in a positive, nonthreatening manner.

It behooves the library media supervisor to let supervisors in other subject areas know what they should expect of the library media program in the schools. The English supervisor does not automatically know there is a scope and sequence of library and information skills that can readily integrate with the English curriculum or that the library media specialist can and will teach. It goes back to the experiences the supervisor had with school library media personnel in the past. Even if those experiences were positive, the supervisor still needs to be brought up-to-date. All too often, the specialist in the school is told by the English teacher, "I cannot bring my class into the media center as planned; I am going to be observed by the English supervisor." The library media supervisor needs to communicate to the English supervisor that a lesson in the library media center is appropriate, meets the objectives of the curriculum, and reflects planning, implementing, and assessment by the English teacher working in concert with the media specialist.

In addition to communication with central office personnel, the library media supervisor needs to build relationships with school-based administrators with regard to the library media program. Too frequently, particularly in a large school system, the media supervisor and the principal fail to exchange ideas about successful library media programs, resulting in difficulties for the program within the school. Whenever possible, the library media supervisor and the English supervisor should address groups of school-based administrators together to reinforce the integration aspect of the two programs. One word of caution: Supervisory personnel should not promise things that cannot be delivered. It is extremely important that the school library media specialist understand the goals and objectives of the system and be willing and able to carry them out prior to the supervisor's overt commitment to any plan. Principals and assistant principals are responsible for developing schedules and for the ultimate success of every program in the school; they need to know that there is a program of instruction for library and information skills and that the library media specialist is responsible for teaching those skills along with the classroom teacher. When positive relationships are built and maintained with school-based administrators, program implementation is facilitated and the library media supervisor will be invited to visit all of the school's programs.

The library media supervisor must know the school-based library media personnel—their abilities, their skills, their deficiencies, their needs, and their flexibility. Library media specialists should keep their supervisor informed about their goals and objectives so the supervisor can provide the necessary assistance to achieve those goals. In many senior high schools, the library media specialist is operating without the help of a fellow professional and must be able to communicate with a supervisory staff that understands the frustrations involved. Inservice programs require input from the school library media specialist, and the supervisor needs to solicit that input. Inservice programs can be planned jointly where library media specialists and English teachers are the facilitators, along with a group of their peers. Planning and learning together is an efficient and valuable use of precious time. Members of the supervisory staff should let the library media specialists know when compliments about specific programs have been made by inservice participants, principals, parents, fellow teachers, or students; a brief e-mail message or written memorandum will communicate to the specialist that someone is paying attention to their efforts.

In many school districts throughout the country, the population and area served are small enough so that the library media supervisor personally knows most members of the community. Whether the district is large or small, however, the library media supervisor should welcome opportunities to address any community group such as the Parent-Student-Teacher Association, a Citizens' Advisory Council, the Rotary Club, or the Friends of the Public Library. Any positive interaction with the community on behalf of the school library media program should be encouraged. Many districts seek to involve community members in the review and evaluation process in selecting library media materials or as volunteers in the school program. These individuals can be strong advocates for the school library media program. If they can see that every effort is being made to deliver instruction of library and information skills through an integrated program and that an effective job is being done in educating young people in the community, a network for positive public relations is established.

When one thinks of library service and the community, the first thing that comes to mind is the public library system. The public library is a rich source to be tapped by the school system. The library media supervisor can set the tone for the relationships between the two institutions. The director of the public libraries in the district and the library media supervisor can confer about common problems and seek solutions. One such example exists in many school districts in Maryland, where the public libraries

provide the school library media centers with access to the Internet through their systems. This kind of cooperation does not exist without a long history of good relationships being established by the leaders of the respective organizations.

What kinds of scheduling can be developed so that the local public librarian can know when the senior English class will be coming in to work on a research topic? How can the two institutions work together to plan for professional growth? What kinds of changes are occurring in the English (or social studies or science) curriculum that will affect the public library? What networks are available through the public library that the school library media specialist should know about and be able to use? These are but a sampling of the issues that the two leaders should discuss in order to make the best possible use of the services that are available.

The library media supervisor needs to communicate with the central office administrative personnel, which includes the superintendent's staff, the director of curriculum, the finance director, and anyone else in a decision-making position. Public relations skills are essential if the library media program is to get a liberal share of the budget and support from the key people in any school system. If the library media supervisor can effectively communicate that the library media program not only supports the entire curriculum offered in the district, but also takes a primary role in teaching library and information skills through an integrated curriculum process, then a firm base is established for seeking support from the decision makers in the system.

The local school board should be included when one considers decision makers in a school system. These people are crucial when it comes to support for new technologies and the necessary training involved for personnel. Invite school board members and central office administrators to see an English class using the available technology in an outstanding library media program. Encourage them to try the CD-ROMs and surf the Internet with students doing the assisting. In many instances these people are not familiar with the capabilities of the computer; they need to know, and students are ideal teachers if they have been taught the appropriate information-seeking skills. The school board and administrators should be informed when the efforts of the library media program in a particular school have been an important factor in improved SAT scores. They should be informed when a student has done an outstanding piece of research in an English class using the resources in the library media center and the public library system. These same educational professionals and advocates should also be informed when a library media program begins to deteriorate as a result of inadequate support.

It is usually the library media supervisor who makes contact with the library media personnel at the state level. The local library media supervisor then has the responsibility to communicate this pertinent information to the specialist in the school. State-level library media personnel have the responsibility for establishing program guidelines, and they become liaisons with local districts for implementation of those guidelines. The state library media supervisor can provide contact with other state supervisory personnel—the state English supervisor, for example—and can also determine trends on a statewide basis. Through state offices, the local supervisor can make contact with other district supervisors and communicate needs, problems, and successful strategies. If professionals in leadership positions at the state level interpret and encourage library and information skills in terms of integrated instruction, that influence will be felt in the local district and, more importantly, in the individual school building. State library media services personnel seek input from the local supervisors, and often professional growth opportunities can be arranged through this vital source to further develop the expertise of the school-based specialists. The district library media supervisor can make other local subject area supervisors aware of services offered through state services, such as access to a professional library, computer networks for review and evaluation for all subjects, curriculum guides from a variety of districts across the country, and timely advice about equipment, including computer technology and software. The implications for

working with state-based library media personnel are monumental in terms of communication and cooperation.

In addition to state-based library media personnel, there are the various organizations that can provide material to help in the process of integrating library media skills into the English curriculum. The American Library Association (ALA) and the American Association of School Librarians (AASL) produce many valuable materials. There are smaller groups within the two affiliates that address the process of instruction in the nation's school library media centers. One such group is the Library Instruction Round Table, which speaks to the bibliographic instructional needs of the librarians and media specialists at every level. The Association for Educational Communication and Technology (AECT) is a vital association for the library media program. In addition, there is the National Council of Teachers of English (NCTE), which is the organization for, by, and about English teachers. The International Reading Association (IRA) is another organization for teachers of English and reading. (See Appendix A for contact and meeting information on these associations.) Just as AASL and AECT cooperated in developing *Information Power: Guidelines for School Library Media Programs*, so did NCTE and IRA cooperate in the development of *Standards for the English Language Arts*. There is no rule that says the library media supervisor cannot belong to the organizations designed for the English and reading teachers. In fact, it would be advantageous to belong to the appropriate organizations and benefit from the many newsletters, home pages, journals, and conferences that these organizations provide over the course of a year. The benefits would far outweigh the amount spent for the membership; the media supervisor could talk intelligently and with authority about current trends in the English program. Belonging to the organization of a fellow instructional leader lends validity to the role of the library media supervisor and sets an example that speaks of the interweaving of instructional roles.

There are usually local organizations to which the library media supervisor should belong that would include public library and school library media groups, as well as English teachers' and reading teachers' associations. At the minimum, the library media supervisor should contact other instructional counterparts to be certain that the various publications from these groups are shared, along with Internet addresses. National concerns usually reflect local concerns, and one can take advantage of solutions to problems that may not have arrived at one's local district, or take solace in the fact that other areas of the country are experiencing similar problems to those in one's own area. These organizations exist for the benefit of their members and there is a wealth of information to be gleaned from them. E-mail can connect the supervisor to the expert in English across town or around the globe. The knowledge gleaned can be shared with others in the local district and can serve as a model to promote relationships and cooperation. Such organizations are extremely valuable resources for the library media supervisor and the district library media program.

 ## The School Library Media Specialist and the English Department

The involvement of the English department chairperson is an essential factor in making the process of integrated skills instruction work at the school level. It is important to gain the confidence of this individual and to let him or her know the possibilities that exist for the English program in the library media center. Prior to any discussion with the English department chairperson, it is necessary for the library media specialist to have a good grasp of the various components of the English curriculum as it is taught in that particular school. One must keep in mind that when curriculum is written at the district level, the schools within the district may not teach every course that is described in the curriculum guide. The rationale for this is that offerings depend upon the school community, the specific school population, the strengths and limitations of the particular English department, and the number of students who are required or elect to take the course. It is imperative that the library media specialist be familiar with the school's schedule and know exactly what English courses are being offered and when they are taught. Further, the specialist should know the course descriptions and the basic content of each course. He or she needs to know the personnel who are teaching the courses and the library media resources that can provide necessary support. In addition, a copy of the instructional program for library and information skills should be available for the chairperson. With these things firmly in mind or in hand, the agenda for a meeting with the English department chairperson should include:

1. Schedule:

   - Are there any changes in the schedule with regard to when courses are being taught and by whom?

   - Where can the library media specialist most logically plug into the schedule for media center orientation with the incoming freshman class?

   - Which courses will require research projects, and approximately when will these projects need to be scheduled in the center?

- What classes would logically need to schedule the computer laboratory, television, or other kinds of production facilities within the school building that may come under the jurisdiction of the library media center?
- Can a schedule be established in advance to assure that the students will get what they need from district services when they can make the most effective use of those services?
- Is it possible to send a tentative schedule of research projects to the public library to help that institution prepare for the inevitable onslaught of students who have a project due tomorrow or next week?
- Are there group activities that need to be scheduled for the media center at the same time and what provisions can be made in advance for those needs in terms of space, resources, and personnel?

2. Goals and Objectives:

- What is the English department chairperson's interpretation of the objectives of the English department in this school, based on the state guidelines, national standards, and district goals?
- How can the goals and objectives for the library media program mesh with these interpretations?
- How can the two departments work together to achieve those goals?
- What kinds of activities were completed successfully in the past by the two departments? Unsuccessfully?
- What can be done by the library media specialist to improve services and assist in meeting those goals and objectives?
- What kinds of inservice training would be helpful to offer to some or all teachers in the English department?

3. Resources:

- What resources are available in the school library media center to support the offerings of the English department?
- What resources need to be reserved through district services—for example, a film or videocassette library?
- What resources will need to be obtained from the community? Public library? What production services are available from the district or outside sources?
- Are there activities that could take advantage of a file of speakers from the community, and can these individuals be scheduled in advance?
- How can microcomputers housed in the media center best be scheduled for use by English classes (considering CD-ROM use, Internet searching, and word processing capabilities)?

4. Activities:

- What activities are planned to utilize the equipment available for producing student projects (cameras, cassette recorders, copiers, computers, etc.)?

- What activities are planned that will use library media center space and personnel?

- What role can the library media specialist fill in assessing those activities that make heavy use of media center services?

- What kinds of instruction from library media services will be needed?

- What classes will be required to do supplemental reading, and what reserve collections or bibliographic assistance will be needed?

This list is by no means exhaustive, but it is a starting point for dialogue between the library media specialist and the English department chairperson. The questions themselves let the chairperson know that the library media center is a force to be reckoned with!

The purpose of any discussion with the department chairperson is to create a relationship that will foster student and faculty use of the library media center by members of the English department. The chairperson becomes the catalyst through whom the library media specialist can work to reach other teachers in the department. It is crucial that the library media specialist speak with every teacher in the department to offer services and library and information skills instruction to students. To be realistic, it may be possible to reach only a few teachers in a department who can be convinced to try an integrated teaching package, but word will spread with each successful experience and relationships will become established. In order to accomplish these successful experiences, another component of good public relations comes into play—careful planning.

In his book, *Managing the Building-Level School Library Media Program*, Warren B. Hicks lists seven steps to be used in any planning process.

1. Identify the problems and recognize opportunities.

2. Set initial objectives.

3. Determine the planning premises—frame the appropriate courses of action, examine data, examine objectives and their alternatives, select the best alternatives for implementation, and decide on courses of action to meet these objectives.

4. Review the alternative courses of action—all courses of action should be investigated.

5. Evaluate each course of action in terms of problems to be solved and objectives to be achieved.

6. Select a plan of action to be implemented.

7. Implement the plan (Hicks 1981, 17).

In reference to the final step in the planning process, Hicks writes: "The total management process comes into play at this step and the media manager uses all of the functions, tools and techniques available to construct the support and implementation systems to carry out the plan." He also stresses the importance of evaluating the plan after it is implemented and revising it as necessary (Hicks 1981, 17).

The importance of good planning cannot be overstated. Obviously there are times when creative things occur spontaneously, but given the workloads carried by the English teacher and the media specialist, the chances for such occurrences are rare because they simply will not fit into crowded schedules.

Time should be made for a library media orientation session with all staff members who are new to the school. The new English teacher needs to know the kinds of services that are readily obtainable from the school library media center and through district services. Welcoming the new member of the staff and introducing him or her to the media center can provide the media specialist with a golden opportunity to demonstrate ways in which library and information skills can be integrated into the curriculum; the new person is most likely to respond positively to the offer of non-threatening help. It is equally important to plan carefully with the English teachers who will be teaching students who are new to the school. An orientation schedule can be established that will allow time for assessing every student's entry level in library and information skills. Even when a school system is fortunate enough to have a well-established scope and sequence of library and information skills, it is important to know exactly what needs to be retaught, reviewed, and introduced. Students become quickly bored and teachers become impatient when students are taught things they already know and know well. On the other hand, nothing is quite as frustrating

as working with students who the library media specialist has erroneously assumed have the necessary prerequisite skills. The instructor may as well be speaking to the students in an unknown language. Planning with the English teacher to pretest all incoming students in the area of library and information skills is essential to a successful program.

In addition to discussing the library media program with the English department chairperson, the library media specialist would be well-advised to discuss schedules, goals and objectives, resources, and activities with each teacher in the English department. It should be encouraging to note that once this has taken place with positive results, ongoing professional relationships will not require inordinate amounts of time. Brief communications to keep each other updated are usually adequate. The English teacher should have realistic expectations of the library media program, and it is easier if those expectations can be established before the fact. For example, the English department should know that the library media center seldom purchases more than several copies of the same title, therefore it is inappropriate to expect more than two or three students to check out the same title from the school's media center at the same time without first talking with the media specialist. It is possible that the library media specialist could borrow additional copies from other school media centers and the public library, if there is enough notice of the need. The English teacher must understand that the collection does not hold thirty copies of *The Color Purple* or any other book used as a text in the English class. Perhaps it would be beneficial for the English teacher to know that the library media center does have many different titles about African Americans and their struggle for equality, and a bibliography on the subject can be prepared quickly with the use of the automated catalog.

With the library media center's access to the Internet or one of the wide variety of online reference systems and CD-ROMs for use with the computer, the English teacher should know that students need to be taught search strategies for successful information retrieval. Time must be allotted for a student to do a search and to evaluate the information accessed. When doing research, students are almost programmed to accept the first hit with a key word and not to look any further, regardless of the source. He or she must learn to evaluate the information found and then check the authority of the provider of the information. The technology that accompanies the computer is expanding faster and faster, providing the school library media program with unlimited access to information. Just as students had to learn that everything that appeared on the printed page or on the television screen was not always fact, so must they learn that everything accessed from the Internet is not necessarily factual. And, students need to be reminded again and again that copying from a Web site is still plagiarism unless proper credit is given to the author. As computers do more and more for us, educators must make every effort to imbue students with a sense of responsibility as they work with this ever-growing technology. Communication and planning are significant considerations for the library media specialist and the teacher when assignments require any library media resource, including the computer and its components.

## The Library Media Specialist and School Administrators

In order for any school library media program to be successful, the library media specialist must build good relationships with the school-based administration. The principal of the high school needs to be informed about any integrated instruction efforts, especially where information skills are taught. He or she is responsible for the overall success of the instructional program within the school and certainly deserves to know about initiatives that have promise for improving student learning outcomes. The principal can be invited to visit the media center when an English class is working on a research project and could be taken through the process by several students. Perhaps there is a need for more computers to serve many purposes. If the principal sees the media center computers being put to good use, then the needed support can be assured—or at least recognized.

I have learned through many years of classroom and library media center experiences that administrators do not like surprises—even good surprises. This does not mean that every minutia related to library media must be carried to the principal's office; instead, a monthly report of activities and happenings in the media center consisting of no more that one page or less can keep him or her apprised of what is occurring. If the library media supervisor has provided in-service training in *Information Problem Solving: The Big Six Skills™ Approach to Library and Information Skills Instruction* (Eisenberg and Berkowitz 1989), and the media specialist is going to use this strategy for the instruction taking place in the media center, the principal needs to be informed and to review the program. When media orders arrive in the center and the media specialist spots an article in a magazine or any other item that might be of interest to the principal, a copy can be made and sent to the office. The same should hold true for faculty members; a magazine article can be copied and placed in the individual's mailbox with a short, "thought you would be interested" note that indicates the shared information is from the media specialist. The title of a new book can be placed in the mailbox or e-mail with an invitation to visit the center. This frequently proves to be a good way to promote library media services to those teachers who do not make much use of the center. When they see what is available, they may return with a class.

The media specialist and the principal need to discuss such questions as: What time elements must be built into a schedule if there is going to be a serious attempt to integrate library and information skills into English and other curricula? How can planning time be arranged to suit both the library media specialist and the members of the English department if skills must be matched at the school level? Can additional clerical help be made available? The library media specialist must know the principal's expectations for the media center and try to accomplish them while reinforcing the role of the library media specialist as information specialist, teacher, and instructional consultant.

 ## The Library Media Specialist and the Public Library

Following the lead from the library media supervisor in the district, the school library media specialist must reach out to the staff in the nearest branch of the public library. The needs of the English department can be effectively communicated at this time, especially those needs that require reserve collections or have time constraints. The public librarian can be invited to the school library media center for an orientation session and take the opportunity to discuss common goals and problems and discover ways in which the two services can best accommodate the school population. The school library media specialist should be well acquainted with the resources, the hours of service, the rules and regulations, and the personnel at the local branch of the public library. That information can be communicated to the staff and students in the school to assist in making their contacts with the public librarian even more beneficial. The specialist can use the steps suggested in Hicks's planning model to provide a duality of service for the school.

School-based library media personnel should build relationships with all of the groups mentioned in this chapter: the community, the state department of education, and various central office personnel, as appropriate. The important thing is for the specialist to stress the positive image of library media services within the school, particularly as the specialist proceeds with the integration of library and information skills into a particular facet of the curriculum.

It is not the intent of this book to illustrate all of the ways in which the student should be reached by the library media specialist. But it should be noted that the student is considered in everything the specialist does. After all, the purpose of the school is to provide learning opportunities for students, and students and learning are why library media specialists, teachers, principals, and supervisors sought jobs in the world of education. Every professional relationship created by the library media specialist should be for the benefit of the students. The specialist should never be so busy with the tactics of the job as to forget the reason for being there in the first place.

As the library media supervisors and specialists work at building relationships through clear communication, careful planning, and other components of a public relations program, they clear the way for delivering an integrated program of library and information skills and the English curriculum.

# Resources for Building Relationships

American Association of School Librarians and Association for Educational Communications and Technology. 1988. *Information Power: Guidelines for School Library Media Programs.* Chicago: American Library Association.

Blake, Barbara Radke, and Barbara L. Stein. 1992. *School and Public Librarians.* New York: Neal-Schuman.

Childress, Valerie. 1993. *Winning Friends for the School Library: A P.R. Handbook.* Worthington, Ohio: Linworth.

Farmer, Lesley S. J. 1995. *Leadership Within the School Library and Beyond.* Worthington, Ohio: Linworth.

Field, Selma G., and Edwin M. Field. 1993. *Publicity Manual for Librarians: A Comprehensive Professional Guide to Communication: A Book No Library Should Be Without.* Monticello, N.Y.: Knowledge and Network Press.

Hamilton, Feona. 1990. *Infopromotion: Publicity and Marketing Ideas for the Information Profession.* Brookfield, Vt.: Ashgate.

Hartzell, George N. 1994. *Building Influence for the School Librarian.* Worthington, Ohio: Linworth.

Haycock, Ken. 1990. *Program Advocacy: Power, Publicity, and the Teacher-Librarian.* Littleton, Colo.: Libraries Unlimited.

Wasman, Ann. 1996. *Ideas for Promoting Your School Library Media Program.* Chicago: American Library Association.

# Chapter 5

# Standards, Guidelines, Frameworks, and Outcomes

The purpose of this chapter is to look at some of the national and state documents that have been created to assist the districts and individual schools as curriculum is being written and delivered. These documents use a variety of terms to explain their purpose and include standards, guidelines, frameworks, and outcomes. A *standard* is defined in most dictionaries as an accepted or acknowledged measure of comparison for qualitative or quantitative values. A synonym would be *criterion* or *norm*. A *guideline* can be defined as a policy issued by an individual or group having authority over a particular activity, and *framework* implies a skeletal support used as the basis for something being constructed. An *outcome* is the consequence or the result of an action. All of these terms relate to the process of learning and teaching, and in this instance, specifically to the English program and library information skills instruction.

##  Standards for the English-Language Arts

The first document to be perused here is *Standards for the English Language Arts*, written by the National Council of Teachers of English (NCTE) and the International Reading Association (IRA) and published in 1996. It is described as a set of content standards for the English-language arts with content standards being defined as "statements that define what students should know and be able to do in the English-language arts." This document goes beyond content and into "purpose, development, and context—and emphasizes the central role of the learner, whose goals and interests drive the processes of learning" (NCTE and IRA 1996, 2).

The reasons for national standards in the English-language arts are expressed as follows: 1) To prepare students for the literacy demands of today and tomorrow; 2) To present a shared vision of literacy education; and 3) To promote equity and excellence for all. As the third need is explained in the text of the document, it stresses not only the need for students to develop specific competencies and to acquire knowledge, but to have the opportunity to reflect on the learning process itself—"the conscious process of learning how to learn. . ." (NCTE and IRA 1996, 2). The entire set of standards is indeed learning centered and is presented as a learning-centered model.

The introductory piece to the standards and the standards appear on pp. 41-42. *Standards for the English Language Arts,* by the International Reading Association and the National Council of Teachers of English, Copyright 1996 by the International Reading Association and the National Council of Teachers of English. Reprinted with permission.

# Introduction to Standards

The vision guiding these standards is that all students must have the opportunities and resources to develop the language skills they need to pursue life's goals and to participate fully as informed, productive members of society. These standards assume that literacy growth begins before children enter school as they experience and experiment with literacy activities—reading and writing, and associating spoken words with their graphic representations. Recognizing this fact, these standards encourage the development of curriculum and instruction that make productive use of the emerging literacy abilities that children bring to school. Furthermore, the standards provide ample room for the innovation and creativity essential to teaching and learning. They are not prescriptions for particular curriculum or instruction.

Although we present these standards as a list, we want to emphasize that they are not distinct and separable; they are, in fact, interrelated and should be considered as a whole.

1. Students read a wide range of print and nonprint texts to build an understanding of texts, of themselves, and of the cultures of the United States and the world; to acquire new information; to respond to the needs and demands of society and the workplace; and for personal fulfillment. Among these texts are fiction and nonfiction, classic and contemporary works.

2. Students read a wide range of literature from many periods in many genres to build an understanding of the many dimensions (e.g., philosophical, ethical, aesthetic) of human experience.

3. Students apply a wide range of strategies to comprehend, interpret, evaluate, and appreciate texts. They draw on their prior experience; their interactions with other readers and writers, their knowledge of word meaning and of other texts, their word identification strategies, and their understanding of textual features (e.g., sound-letter correspondence, sentence structure, context, graphics).

4. Students adjust their use of spoken, written, and visual language (e.g., conventions, style, vocabulary) to communicate effectively with a variety of audiences and for different purposes.

5. Students employ a wide range of strategies as they write and use different writing process elements appropriately to communicate with different audiences for a variety of purposes.

6. Students apply knowledge of language structure, language conventions (e.g., spelling and punctuation), media techniques, figurative language, and genre to create, critique, and discuss print and nonprint texts.

7.  Students conduct research on issues and interests by generating ideas and questions, and by posing problems. They gather, evaluate, and synthesize data from a variety of sources (e.g., print and nonprint texts, artifacts, people) to communicate their discoveries in ways that suit their purpose and audience.

8.  Students use a variety of technological and informational resources (e.g., libraries, databases, computer networks, video) to gather and synthesize information and to create and communicate knowledge.

9.  Students develop an understanding of and respect for diversity in language use, patterns, and dialects across cultures, ethnic groups, geographical regions, and social roles.

10. Students whose first language is not English make use of their first language to develop competency in the English language arts and to develop understanding of content across the curriculum.

11. Students participate as knowledgeable, reflective, creative, and critical members of a variety of literacy communities.

12. Students use spoken, written, and visual language to accomplish their own purposes (e.g., for learning, enjoyment, persuasion, and the exchange of information) (NCTE and IRA 1996, 3).

Chapter 3 of the standards document gives thought and further explanation to each of the standards listed with continued emphasis upon the interrelationship among them. This chapter reinforces the belief that the standards should speak to a "consensus growing out of actual classroom practices and, not be a prescriptive framework." Also, the equity issue is raised, particularly as it relates to standard Number 8—student use of "a variety of technological and informational resources." It states:

> Electronic technologies, perhaps more than any other recent innovation, have heightened our sense of the need for reform and have raised our expectations of what students must know and be able to do in English language arts. It is therefore crucial that we address the uneven distribution of technology in our nation's schools. Some schools have abundant computers for students to use, while others have only a few, which are often reserved for the students regarded as academically advanced. Students in economically disadvantaged communities and those labeled as less proficient often lack access to new technologies or are confined to routine computer activities that fail to challenge and develop their minds. Schools and communities need to address these inequities to ensure that all students can become technologically literate" (NCTE and IRA 1996, 40-41).

Every educator knows this is all too true, but strong efforts are being made to correct those inequities from the federal level to the individual schoolhouse itself. Another aspect of the technology crunch that is stressed in this section of the standards is the fact that many teachers are not comfortable with the technology and have not had adequate opportunities for staff development in order to become more familiar with it. One finds oneself in the unique situation where the student becomes the teacher and the teacher learns terms and techniques about the computer from the student. This reversal of roles should be welcomed and looked upon as an opportunity for the student to increase his or her self-esteem.

Chapter 4 is titled "Standards in the Classroom" and consists of vignettes for each level of school—elementary, middle, and secondary—taken from actual classroom practices. Many examples of interdisciplinary learning are given, and the reader is encouraged to seek out connections to help students increase their literacy in a number of subjects. With regard to how well the students are learning and to what extent the standards are being met, it states: "Judgments . . . need to be made by those who see them working with language every day. In response to questions about how progress toward the standards is to be evaluated, we strongly affirm the role of the teacher. By watching students closely, reflecting on their development, and guiding them when they need help, teachers both assess and advance their students' progress" (NCTE and IRA 1996, 67).

*Standards for the English Language Arts* is a document that should be available in every high school library media center, along with national standards from every other discipline. The library media specialist needs to be familiar with the document and be able to discuss the content with knowledge and comprehension. There are many places where the English standards can be part of integrated instruction.

 ## Information Power: Guidelines for School Library Media Programs

The comparable document to *Standards for the English Language Arts* for the school library media program is *Information Power: Guidelines for School Library Media Programs*, published in 1988 and revised in 1998 with the title *Information Power: Building Partners for Learning*.

*Information Power* presents its vision in the form of five challenges; challenges that have the capacity to alter dramatically the kinds of services school library media specialists offer, the facility in which they work, and even the profession itself.

Challenge 1. To provide intellectual and physical access to information and ideas for a diverse population whose needs are rapidly changing.

Challenge 2. To ensure equity and freedom of access to information and ideas, unimpeded by social, cultural, economic, geographic, or technological constraints.

Challenge 3. To promote literacy and the enjoyment of reading, viewing, and listening for young people at all ages and stages of development.

Challenge 4. To provide leadership and expertise in the use of information and instructional technologies.

Challenge 5. To participate in networks that enhance access to resources located outside the school (AASL and AECT 1988).

# Library Media Program Objectives

Each of these challenges is accompanied by the influences that have produced the challenges and the implications that will surely have an impact upon the job of the library media specialist. (Indeed the library media specialist has been faced with these implications over the last decade, and continues to deal with the challenges proffered in *Information Power*.) The mission of the library media program is succinctly stated: "The mission of the library media program is to ensure that students and staff are effective users of ideas and information" (AASL and AECT 1988, 1). Following the mission statement, a number of specific objectives are listed.

1. To provide intellectual access to information through systematic learning activities which develop cognitive strategies for selecting, retrieving, analyzing, evaluating, synthesizing, and creating information at all age levels and in all curriculum content areas.

2. To provide physical access to information through (a) a carefully selected and systematically organized collection of diverse learning resources, representing a wide range of subjects, levels of difficulty, communication formats, and technological delivery systems; (b) access to information and materials outside the library media center and the school building through such mechanisms as interlibrary loan, networking and other cooperative agreements, and on-line searching of databases; and (c) providing instruction in the operation of equipment necessary to use the information in any format.

3. To provide learning experiences that encourage users to become discriminating consumers and skilled creators of information through introduction to the wide range of communications media and use of the new and emerging information technologies.

4. To provide leadership, instruction, and consulting assistance in the use of instructional and information technology and the use of sound instructional design principles.

5. To provide resources and activities that contribute to lifelong learning while accommodating a wide range of differences in teaching and learning styles and in instructional methods, interests, and capacities.

6. To provide a facility that functions as the information center of the school, as a locus for integrated, interdisciplinary, intergrade, and school-wide learning activities.

7. To provide resources and learning activities that represent a diversity of experiences, opinions, social and cultural perspectives, supporting the concept that intellectual freedom and access to information are prerequisite to effective and responsible citizenship in a democracy (AASL and AECT 1988, 1–2).

In ensuing chapters of *Information Power*, guidelines are given for the school library media program, planning, and management as it relates to the media center; recommendations for personnel at the school and district levels; guidelines for resources, equipment, and facilities; and delineation of the responsibilities for school library media services for the district, region, and state. Appendices provide details and explanations of the information provided in the text.

As one examines these two documents, it becomes obvious that the English-language arts standards are written with the accent placed on what the student is expected to accomplish through his or her work with the English-language arts teacher. The school library media guidelines stress the role of the library media specialist and the challenges that must be addressed in order to provide a broad range of information capabilities to the learner, whether the learner is a student, teacher, administrator, or a member of the community. Even though the emphasis is different in each document, there is considerable common ground: the recognition of our diverse population and the various needs therein; the provision of experiences that enable the student to collect, evaluate, and synthesize data from a number of resources; the promotion of literacy involving reading, viewing, and listening; and instruction in the use and evaluation of technological and informational resources. There are other areas where the two national documents cross paths. The ultimate aim of both is to provide a guide for the best practices in the individual professions, to address the inequities that exist in our nation's schools, and to prepare our students for life in the twenty-first century.

 ## Maryland's Standards, Curricular Framework, and Outcomes for School Library Media Programs

The Maryland State Department of Education, School Library Media Services Branch, has provided school districts in the state with strong leadership for decades. This leadership goes back to Mae I. Graham who was appointed as the first Maryland state supervisor of school libraries following World War II. Miss Graham's emphasis was to place libraries and librarians in schools and to encourage those librarians to teach library skills and to promote the appreciation of reading and literature to Maryland's students. That solid tradition has continued through good and bad economic times, depletion of state department staff (and increased responsibilities), and the multitude of influences that have affected education in general since the late 1940s. There are many other states that can claim this same strong leadership.

### Standards for School Library Media Programs in Maryland

In 1984 the Maryland State Board of Education adopted Resolution No. 1984-12, "Statement of Purpose for School Library Media Programs in Maryland," committing itself to vigorous support of school library media programs. The Board directed that a committee revise and develop specific criteria and standards for school library media programs in Maryland. The "Statement of Purpose" forms the introduction to *Standards for School Library Media Programs in Maryland*.

The unified school library media program is essential to effective education for an information based society. A unified school library media program is designed to support the educational goals of a school system and to serve all students and teachers. Such a program is accomplished by providing both an organized collection of materials and instruction in the use of those materials as an integrated part of the total educational program. In order to support fully the instructional program, appropriate materials and equipment of various types and formats must be centrally managed in the school library media center. An effective unified school library media program requires adequate professional and support staff.

A school library media program is an integral part of the instructional process. This integration is most effective when appropriate professional library media personnel participate in the development and implementation of educational programs. The school library media specialist, in cooperation with other teachers, instructs students in those library, research, and study skills which have been integrated into all areas of the curriculum.

School library media programs do not duplicate those of public and other library programs. School library media services support specific instructional programs, complement instruction in reading and critical thinking skills and habits, and have knowledge and information on site immediately available for specific purposes. Further, school library media programs serve a specific segment of the total population and are administered by certificated school library media specialists. School library media personnel cooperate with personnel in public and other types of libraries in order to expand access to available resources (MSDE 1987, 1).

Permission to reprint from the *Standards for School Library Media Programs in Maryland* has been granted by School Library Media Services, Maryland State Department of Education.

The Statement of Purpose continues by giving the components of a successful unified school library media program. Those components are given the following headings: program, personnel, resources, facility, instruction, and resource services. It is upon this Statement of Purpose and the accompanying components of a successful library media program that the *Standards for School Library Media Programs in Maryland* is based. The document is arranged so that each standard embraces a list of criteria to be used to evaluate the extent to which the standard has been accomplished in an individual school. The criteria statements are to be checked yes or no, or left blank. Supportive evidence is required to validate the rating given by the school library media program. The following scale is used for rating each standard:

O = Not Started used when all criteria statements are checked no.

W = Working Toward when criteria statements are checked both yes and no.

I = Implemented when all criteria statements are checked yes.

NA = Not Applicable when criteria statements are viewed as irrelevant or not applicable (MSDE 1987, 3).

The process used for the in-school evaluation is similar to that used by the National Study of School Evaluation in that an advisory committee is formed consisting of a variety of school- and community-based people and, along with the school library media staff, a rating is given to each standard. It behooves the library media specialist to have appropriate documentation available to substantiate the ratings. The document is signed by the principal and the media specialist and turned in to the library media supervisor at the district level. The information gathered is compiled, and the degree of compliance with the *Standards* document is assessed. The Maryland State Department of Education examines the information from each school district every four years and the compiled data is used for a variety of purposes, including requests for additional resources, staff development, and ultimately, reporting to the state board of education the state of the school library media programs within Maryland.

## The seven standards are:

1.0 Philosophy—The school library media program has a written philosophy which is consistent with the educational philosophy of the school and the library media philosophy of the local education agency and the state.

2.0 Goals and Objectives—The school library media program has written goals and objectives related to the overall school library media philosophy.

3.0 Instruction–3.1 Direct Instruction—The library media staff instructs students in location, selection, utilization, appreciation, and production skills. The teaching of these skills is effective when integrated into the educational program.

3.2 Support of Instruction—The library media staff assists in the support of instruction by providing services.

4.0 Staffing—The size of the local school system and scope of library media services will determine the number of central office and school library media staff members. Regardless of the number of schools in a local system, certain resources and services should be provided by a central staff working out of the system-level library media center under the direction of a certificated library media administrator.

5.0 Resources and Resource Services—The school library media program is organized to provide resources and resource services to students and staff.

6.0 Facilities—Each local education agency should designate conveniently located and barrier-free space in each school for provision of library media services.

7.0 Program Evaluation—Each local education agency and school should have a formally adopted a comprehensive plan for evaluating all levels and aspects of school library media programs (MSDE 1987).

Each standard lists specific criteria, along with examples of documentation, which must be rated according to the previously explained scale. Most school library media specialists in Maryland maintain a file for each standard and keep documentation current in order to complete the required ratings each year. The advisory committee that reviews these standards should remain active to serve as a sounding board for the evaluation process, as well as provide advice on many issues that confront the media specialist.

### The Library Media Program: A Maryland Curricular Framework

In 1991, the Maryland State Department of Education published *Library Media Program: A Maryland Curricular Framework* to serve as a companion piece to subject area curricular frameworks. This document was developed by a committee consisting of school-based media specialists and teachers from all levels, media and subject-area supervisors, and school administrators, including a district superintendent. In the introduction to the framework, the statement of purpose tells the user that the document is "designed to assist Maryland library media administrators and specialists in planning, developing, and implementing K through 12 library media programs. It provides a broad outline from which local systems may construct library media programs integrated with other curricular units" (MSDE 1991, 21). The intent of this document is to help local systems as they plan to develop curriculum, to develop a local philosophy, to define a set of goals and objectives, to develop a scope and sequence, to evaluate the current curriculum documents with regard to outcomes, and to identify necessary curricular content and teaching strategies. The *Library Media Program: A Maryland Curricular Framework* is based entirely on Standard 3.0, Instruction, from *Standards for School Library Media Programs in Maryland*. It includes the major purposes of direct library media instruction and is intended to cross all grade levels. Nine goals are stated; the first five develop the skills needed for students to succeed in an information age; goals six through eight stress the importance of positive attitudes toward books and other media and their creators; and goal nine focuses on student production. They are listed on page 49.

# Library Media Program Goals

Goal 1.    focuses on the location, organization, and utilization of the materials and equipment in a school media center. Effective use of the school library media center requires an understanding of its classification system, the characteristics of different media, a demonstrated knowledge of services offered, and appropriate handling of materials and equipment.

Goal 2.    focuses on the effective review, evaluation, and selection of media for an identified information need. Through examination of established criteria, the most appropriate resource can be obtained.

Goal 3.    focuses on the effective use of study, research, reference, and critical thinking skills to manage information in order to solve problems. Frequently, these skills are taught in the classroom and reinforced in the school library media center. This goal provides an ideal opportunity to integrate library media skills with skills from other curricula.

Goal 4.    focuses on the application of comprehension skills to acquire desired information from the wide range of media available through the school library media center.

Goal 5.    focuses on the use of technology in the school library media center and other libraries. Information may be accessed readily through electronic sources. Appropriate skills are vital if the information accessed is to serve the intended purpose.

Goal 6.    focuses on the pursuit of reading for pleasure and enrichment. The unique features of special collections, public, and other libraries are explored as extensions of the school library media center.

Goal 7.    focuses on the appreciation of literature as a reflection of, and an influence on, the human experience. The goal relates directly to the *English Language Arts Curricular Framework*, Goal 6. The library media specialist and the English Language Arts teacher have the opportunity to work cooperatively to stimulate appreciation of literature.

Goal 8.    focuses on the value of books and other media as sources of information and recreation. Observance of copyright laws and the promotion of intellectual freedom are recognized as responsibilities in a democratic society.

Goal 9.    focuses on the production of print and nonprint media. The processes used to produce different media are explored and criteria are developed to determine the appropriate medium for a particular purpose (MSDE 1991).

Permission to reprint from the *Library Media Program: A Maryland Curricular Framework* has been granted by School Library Media Services, Maryland State Department of Education.

Each goal is followed by subgoals that further delineate the desired outcomes, and the subgoals are further explained as student-centered expectancies. An example is probably the best way to demonstrate the format used in *Library Media Program: A Maryland Curriculum Framework*. As stated, Goal 7 refers directly to the *English Language Arts Curricular Framework*, Goal 6.

GOAL 7   To appreciate literature.

Subgoal 7.1 To recognize authors, illustrators, publishers, and producers of literature as reflectors of the human experience.

The learner:

7.1.1   identifies the effects of the authors' or illustrators' personal and cultural experiences on their work.

7.1.2   recognizes how authors, producers, and illustrators use a variety of language devices such as symbolism, color, sound, and figurative language to communicate human experiences.

Subgoal 7.2 To recognize that literature reflects, examines, and influences the human experience.

The learner:

7.2.1   uses literature to explore a wide range of human experiences.

7.2.2   recognizes why an author selects one literary form as more effective than another.

Subgoal 7.3 To select from a variety of literary genres and themes.

The learner:

7.3.1   identifies the characteristics of various literary genres and forms.

7.3.2   explores a wide variety of fiction and nonfiction, poetry and prose in print and nonprint formats.

Subgoal 7.4 To participate in literary experiences.

The learner:

7.4.1   relates literary experiences to personal experiences.

7.4.2   uses established criteria to evaluate literature (MSDE 1991, 24).

Examples of district philosophy, goals, and a scope and sequence of skills are included in the document, followed by how to create a curriculum match. In Maryland, the creation of curriculum matches with library media skills was made relatively easy (though time consuming) because every discipline has a curricular framework and the format is essentially the same for each area. This match, then, could be used at the local level with the more specific curricular guide.

## Learning Outcomes

In 1994, the Maryland State Department of Education published *Learning Outcomes in Library Media Skills*, again utilizing the format established by subject area curricula. The goals used in *Library Media Program: A Maryland Curricular Framework* were examined by the committee formed to work with student outcomes, and it was decided to consolidate the nine goals from the document into seven student learning outcomes. The learning outcomes in library media skills are:

- Students will demonstrate the ability to locate and use materials and equipment.
- Students will demonstrate the ability to review, evaluate, and select media for an identified information need.
- Students will demonstrate the ability to learn and apply study, research, reference, and critical thinking skills to organize information.
- Students will demonstrate the ability to comprehend content in various types of media.
- Students will demonstrate the ability to retrieve and manage information.
- Students will demonstrate an appreciation of books and other media as sources of information and recreation.
- Students will demonstrate the ability to create print and nonprint media (MSDE 1993, 2).

Each outcome is buttressed by additional information for the specific skill and/or attitudes addressed in the outcome. Examples of possible curriculum matches are included to emphasize the importance of integrating instruction, as well as demonstrate that the parallel already exists. In order to make the integration work at the district or school level, the media specialist and the subject area teacher need to share their respective documents and decide where integrated instruction can be utilized to assist the learner in accomplishing the stated outcome.

There can be little doubt that standards, guidelines, frameworks, and outcomes serve as helpful conductors as the educator creates and revises curriculum, re-works instructional strategies, and deals with new and faster technologies. In addition to providing assistance in the developmental stage, there is also the assessment aspect to consider. If national standards are available, one can compare what is being done in the classroom or media center to see if those standards are being applied and how well they are being assimilated by the students. State standards give another yardstick to measure what is happening in the schoolhouse and the district against that document. These same tools can be used as public relations vehicles to inform school communities about what ought to be expected of a school library media center. The reason for the existence of any of these documents is to provide assistance to the educator as he or she goes about the business of teaching and managing. It is the responsibility of the supervisory staff to provide the school-based educator with access to these national and state documents or, preferably, to arrange for inservice training in the use of these documents. If there can be thorough understanding of the breadth of thinking that has generated these documents and if teachers and library media specialists explore ways to implement the content, then students are the beneficiaries.

# Chapter 6

## District Library Media Programs

The supervisory staff at the district level has the responsibility to interpret national standards and state guidelines in order to develop a logical curricular program that is compatible with local philosophy. A document defining the district library media program may take various forms; however, a written, school-board-approved version is essential, not only for the school library media specialist and students served, but also as a tool in planning with other supervisors and teachers to integrate library information instruction into the overall program. This same document can be used for public relations purposes to explain the school library media program to administrators, parents, and community leaders.

This chapter provides examples of district level school library media programs to assist in the development of new programs or the revision of existing ones. The library media program encompasses many things: a selection policy; a telecommunications student-use policy; a library media circulation policy; and requirements from the district regarding budgeting, purchasing, processing, and weeding of library media materials and equipment. The program can be contained in a centrally produced procedural manual to be used by the school library media staff as a management and policy guide. The school library media specialist often develops a school-centered handbook that covers all of the information applicable to that particular school media center—such as hours of operation, requirements for circulation, computer use, and any other significant school-based details. This school library media handbook would be distributed to teachers and students to encourage use of the library media center and to clarify district and school policies. While these guides are important parts of the school library media program, this chapter will focus primarily on the library media instructional program and its relationship to students, teachers, and the community.

New technologies need to be integrated with more traditional methods to provide the school library media specialist with appropriate guidelines for instruction. Writing instructional programs requires careful deliberation and thoughtful input from everyone responsible for delivering the program. For example, if the library media curriculum committee has made a decision to pilot a particular model as a part of the instructional program, the committee should garner support from the library media specialists who will be using the model.

The examples used here are taken from Maryland districts where I have observed the actual implementation of the written documents. Often these documents are lengthy and repetitive since the same skills are introduced, reinforced, and finally mastered; therefore, sample portions from two local districts will be used to illustrate different approaches. The first example demonstrates the way in which one system has developed cooperative programs to teach parents and members of the community the technology of the Internet, among other things. The second example is a sampling from a straight-forward, more traditional scope and sequence of school library media skills.

 # Baltimore County Public Schools— Office of Library Information Services

According to statistics from the Office of Communications and Special Projects in Baltimore County Public Schools, this county school system is the 25th largest in the nation. There are 160 schools and an operating budget of $645 million serving more than 105,000 students (Baltimore County Public Schools 1998a). The communities within the county are diverse, and generally speaking, the county population is genuinely interested in the school system. A big asset for those who live, work, and attend school in the county is the Baltimore County Public Library system, one of the largest in the country and an active participant in the community, especially with the schools.

The school library media program in the Baltimore County Public Schools has undergone a series of dramatic changes during the last decade of the twentieth century. When school-based management became the driving force in many school districts in the early 1990s, many so-called "special" teachers, including library media specialists, were removed from the faculty roster in some schools in favor of an additional classroom teacher. This happened in a number of schools in Baltimore County, and aides or teachers

untrained in the library media profession were assigned the task of operating the media centers. If a teacher was assigned to the media center, it was usually as a minimal part of another assignment, such as teaching reading. The aide often had other responsibilities within the school and did not devote full time to the media center. These individuals checked out materials, ordered media, distributed equipment, and tried to keep a semblance of order on the shelves. Interestingly, every senior high school library media center in Baltimore County retained at least one library media specialist during this period of time. The middle schools and the elementary schools were hit the hardest.

## A Cohort Program

It did not take long for administrators and school-based management committees to determine that a certificated school library media specialist did make a difference—a big difference—in the operation of the school. By 1995 library media specialists were in demand again in the county's schools and, unfortunately, an adequate supply of qualified media professionals was not available. Other districts had hired the library media specialists declared excess by Baltimore County. The central office library media staff decided to take positive action to solve the problem and sought ways to attract educational professionals into the library media centers, with proper certification. A cohort program was developed with nearby Towson University's Instructional Technology Program, and teachers were given incentives to go back to school and get their certification as library media specialists. The program is successful and, once again, schools are being staffed with qualified library media specialists. In the midst of this period, after several changes in leadership, the Office of Library and Media Services changed its name to Library Information Services, reflecting a reorganization within the school system.

## Parent Internet Education

The cohort program with Towson University is but one cooperative venture undertaken by the library media personnel in Baltimore County. Many in the library media profession have struggled with ways to train fellow teachers and interested citizens in the use of the Internet. Della Curtis, coordinator of the Office of Library Information Services, and Doris Glotzbach, supervisor, had the responsibility of writing the policy paper regarding student use of the Internet and telecommunications in general—a task which has fallen to district-level personnel in many school systems. As a result of this policy paper, Curtis was invited to attend the White House Online Summit: Focus on Children, in Washington, D.C., in December 1997. At this conference, Vice President Gore announced a plan to build a family-friendly Internet which included involvement of parents to learn more about the Internet, to develop content-specific sites for children, and to enforce existing laws to protect children in cyberspace.

Inspired and encouraged by this national summit, Curtis and her staff developed a program to educate parents and interested citizens from Baltimore County communities in the use of the Internet. The program was approved by the county board of education and titled **P**arent Internet Education, or P.I.E. Sponsors and partners were recruited, with Towson University quickly responding to the challenge. The Baltimore County Public Library system has a long history of cooperation with the school system and was already in the business of training adults to use computers. That institution also offered its services. The Baltimore County Public School Parent Teacher Association became partners with the endeavor, and a number of businesses joined in the challenge.

An ambitious project was planned for parents, and Parry Aftab, esq., the author of *A Parents' Guide to the Internet: And How to Protect Your Children in Cyberspace,* was hired as an on-site project consultant. Following an extensive publicity campaign, the initial sessions were held at Towson University, centrally located in Baltimore County. School library media specialists, along with public librarians and other knowledgeable citizens, were responsible for developing curriculum, then planning and implementing almost all of the sessions. Each school was charged with the task of forming its own local P.I.E. team to address concerns in the home community. The school system's Education Television Channel assisted with the endeavor by using its interactive distance learning system to deliver some of the curriculum as well as a P.I.E. Town Meeting with sites determined by schools that currently offered distance learning courses.

This challenging effort continues to bring positive media response to Baltimore County's school library information program. The local news agencies have praised the project, and there has also been national interest. Obviously this program has generated worthy publicity and focused attention upon the school system's library information program. It has also taken a huge amount of time and effort on the part of the project's providers, but more and more citizens in Baltimore County have begun to see the complexities of the job of the library media specialist. For more information about P.I.E., check the Internet. The Website can be accessed at www.bcplonline.org/online (accessed November 12, 1998).

This chapter will not provide a detailed report about P.I.E., worthy though it is in terms of commitment and outcome. It is included here because it is a district program, basic in its concepts and presentation, and totally applicable to student learning. In many instances, the school media specialists involved in its development and delivery modified materials they had previously implemented in their school media centers as they worked with students and staff. The curriculum package delivered to parents includes the following units:

1. Internet Issues: Understanding the Spirit of the Internet

2. Introduction to the Internet: What Is It?

3. Internet Basics: Surfing the Web

4. Search Engines: How Do I Find What I Want?

5. Email: Person-to-Person Online

6. Everyday Living with the Internet: Useful Websites for Families
   (Baltimore County Public Schools 1998b)

In the first unit, Internet Issues, (see pp. 57–60) one of the big topics is evaluating the sources found on the Internet. Two library media specialists were involved in developing this package, with assistance from other individuals. Ann B. O'Neill, the library media specialist at Franklin High School, and Carrie Everhart, the library media specialist at Catonsville High School, were the leaders of the committee that developed and delivered the evaluation piece. The subject of evaluating materials located on the Internet will be addressed again in this book. Since most media specialists agree it is one of the most difficult ideas for students to grasp and because it is such an important issue, different approaches seem appropriate.

# WHY EVALUATE?

The most difficult and time consuming parts of research used to be the gathering of information. Today, that can be the easiest part, thanks to technology.

### Volume of Resources

The number of resources available via the Internet is immense. In the 1997 *A Parents' Guide to the Internet*, author Parry Aftab states, "there are now 1.1 million separate websites, with millions more sub-pages within those websites." ( By comparison, there were only 130 sites in 1993.)

### Anyone Can Publish on the Internet

Organizations, companies, educational institutions, government agencies, communities, and individual people all serve as information providers for the electronic Internet community. This technology allows anyone to publish anything at anytime—and it's easy to do.

### No Approval Necessary

Most of the information on the Internet is not reviewed or "filtered." In other words, unlike the more traditional information media (books, magazines, videos) which passes through an editor, the content of a web page does not have to be approved by anyone before it is made public. Seldom is there a reviewing process conducted by peers or an authority, or checking by a publisher or editor, or selection by a librarian during collection development. Anyone can say anything. Unfortunately, many people, especially students, often believe "If it's on the Internet, it must be true."

## EVALUATION CRITERIA

Following are some basic criteria for evaluating Internet resources.

## AUTHORITY

Authority indicates whether or not an individual, an organization, or an agency is recognized as an expert in a field and if that body is knowledgeable, qualified, and reliable. An example of a reliable authority would be a university or government agency. Authority is an extremely important criterion when evaluating Internet resources.

- **Author's qualifications and affiliation**—Is the author/information provider clearly identified? Is data included about the author? Is the author affiliated with a recognized organization or institution?

Examine the URL (address) to gain clues to the authority of the source. One part of the URL is the host—a three-letter suffix indicating the type of domain:

**edu**=college or university

**org**=nonprofit organization

**gov**=government agency or organization

**int**=international organization

**mil**=military

**com**=commercial organization

**net**=network provider

In the example **http://www.jhu.edu/~jsmith/sports.html**, edu indicates the host is an educational institution, in this case Johns Hopkins University. This appears to be a reputable example, but the **tilde (~)** after the type of domain usually indicates a personal web page rather than part of the organization's official web site. The example indicates this site is a file about sports in the folder of someone named jsmith. Careful scrutiny should be applied to such sites.

- **Contact person**—Is there a contact person or address available? Can the webmaster be contacted easily?

- **Reliability**—Are sources of information stated? Is the information verifiable?

- **Evidence of quality control**—Is there evidence of quality control?

Many websites do not have anyone overseeing their content; however there are times when information has been reviewed prior to its being published on the Internet. Some examples are:

- Information presented on an official organizational website

- Online journals that use peer review by editors

- Posting of information taken from books or journals that have undergone a process of quality control

**Some websites to check for various aspects of authority:**

Holocaust Controversy

The Holocaust: An Historical Summary

HIV/AIDS Information Center

The True but Little Known Facts About Women and AIDS

## DESIGN AND STYLE

- **User friendly**—Does the site lend itself to ease of use?

- **Consistency**—Is there consistency in basic design formats?

- **Uncluttered and clean**—Are the pages uncluttered and cleanly designed?

- **Basic design must reflect the content**—Do the graphics and art serve a function or are they simply decorative?

**Some sites to evaluate for design and style:**

Salem-Teikyo University

KidsHealth at the AMA

## OBJECTIVITY

Objectivity refers to the presence of factual data and the lack of personal prejudice in the information presented.

- **Evidence of bias**—Is the material presented selectively or in an unbalanced manner? Is only one side of an issue presented? Was some information left out?

- **Soap box**—Is someone merely "sounding off" about an issue or an opinion?

- **Changing opinion**—To what extent is the creator trying to change our opinion?

**Here are some sites to examine for objectivity:**

American Lung Association

R. J. Reynolds

Smoking from All Sides

## CURRENCY

When it comes to currency of information, the Internet can have a definite advantage over traditional information resources. Its technology allows almost instantaneous updating of information. Students can follow the launch of a space shuttle or track a hurricane practically minute by minute.

Be aware that if a date is provided on a site, that date may have various meanings. For example:

- **Date of information**—It may indicate when the material was first written

- **Publication date**—It may indicate when the material was first placed on the web

- **Date of last revision**—It may indicate when the material was last revised

A site may be updated or revised without all of the information being revised. Do the dates for the updates correspond to the information in the resource? Does the organization or person hosting the resource appear to have a commitment to ongoing maintenance and stability of the resource?

Look at the dates and decide what is important and relevant to you. As in printed sources, some work is timeless, like classic novels or much of history. Other work has a limited useful life because of advances in the discipline (as in science, for example) or because it is outdated very quickly (as in technology news). You must therefore be careful to note when the information you retrieve was first created and then decide whether it is still of value.

- **Up-to-date-links**—Are the links to other sites up-to-date? Do they work or are they dead ends? The latter two situations are very frustrating and often make one question the validity of the entire site.

**Here are some examples to check for currency:**

> USA Today
>
> NASA Homepage

## NAVIGATION

Navigation refers to how easy it is to move around a website.

- **Organization**—Is the site organized in a logical manner to facilitate the location of information?
- **Table of contents**—Does the site have a well-labeled table of contents?
- **Consistent buttons**—Are the navigation buttons consistent throughout the website?
- **Clear and accurate links**—Are the links clearly and accurately described?
- **Sufficient links**—Are a sufficient number of links provided?

**Here are some links to sites for evaluating navigation:**

| | |
|---|---|
| WebElements | onLine: on Librarians' Network for Essential Curriculum |
| NASA Homepage | |
| REVIEW! | |

## *Remember . . .*

The Internet is only one source of information.

1. It can be very useful for researching certain topics.

2. It can be almost useless for other topics.

3. To research a topic thoroughly, use a variety of sources—Internet and traditional.

Internet evaluation techniques are just beginning to be developed. Technology is outpacing the ability to create standards and guidelines. Establishing evaluation procedures will be an ongoing, evolutionary process (Baltimore County Public Schools 1998).

One can readily see that this session could be used to teach many different groups, whether it be for those students just beginning to use the Internet, as a review and a reminder to those who are experienced in online research, or for adults who are trying to catch up with their children or students. The other sessions in the program are just as basic and simplistic in approach as this one. The **P**arent **I**nternet **E**ducation or P.I.E. program is one of the first of its kind in terms of including a wide segment of the population in a district as large as Baltimore County. The program is still in its beginning stages, and it will be interesting to follow its progress as citizens claim a "piece of the P.I.E." The Baltimore County Website will provide additional information as the program moves into the future.

## Other Uses of the Internet by and for Baltimore County Schools

The Baltimore County Public Library has developed a Homework Website in conjunction with the Office of Library Information Services. Teachers are encouraged to use the site to fill in an online form for homework assignments to enable students to check assignments from home or from their public library branch, then access subject-specific materials at the library or school media center. Parents can also check the site to verify assignments. Not only is this a good public relations tool, it assists the students who have missed class that day and helps prepare the public library for an onslaught of students all requesting the same materials at the same time. Suggestions are given by both the public librarian, the teacher, and the school media specialist for appropriate materials to use.

Another important use of the Website by the Office of Library Information Services has been to provide a list of specific URLs appropriate to every curriculum area for teachers, kept current by a committee of school library media specialists and also accessible by the community. An enormous amount of time can be saved if the individual seeking information can go directly to an address that has been evaluated and deemed accurate and subject-appropriate. In the same vein,

a synopsis of essential curriculum at each grade level and for every subject is available for students, parents, and the entire community to examine. This, along with the P.I.E. project, has helped to keep the community informed and has lessened concerns about student safety in the use of the Internet. A number of other projects to be placed on the Website are in the planning stage, such as a library information site that includes research modules for each grade level, to be developed by teachers and library media specialists. It should be stated that the Baltimore County Public Library system has provided space for the school system's Websites on its URL. The two systems have cooperated to keep the public abreast about what is happening in both institutions by using technology to encourage the use of libraries and school library media centers.

The Baltimore County model shows just a small piece of the total **P**arent **I**nternet **E**ducation model which is also used (modified as necessary) with students and as inservice training for teachers. Obviously, use of the Internet is only a part of the library information instructional program for students, but it is becoming increasingly important in our schools and in our lives. We are rapidly reaching the point where knowledge of the computer and its capabilities is a requirement for almost any level of work or study.

Of course, there are many other ways to provide for library and information instruction. A scope and sequence of library media skills remains a standard in many school systems. It is easy to use; the library media specialist can look at a specific grade level and know exactly what skills and/or attitudes need to be encouraged, introduced, reinforced, or mastered during a particular year. This method gives the library media specialist a specific tool to use in integrating library information skills with school curriculum. While working with the teacher is always the preferred technique when developing or modifying lessons for the library media program, the reality of that happening with every teacher is not likely. If an effort has been made to match library and information skills with curricular areas at either the school or district levels, then an integrated program can be achieved in the media center.

**Washington County Public Schools'
Scope and Sequence**

Maryland's Washington County is located in the western part of the state and is known for its grand, open spaces and ever-present Blue Ridge Mountains. It is a rapidly developing area and is becoming a bedroom community for Washington, D.C., as well as Baltimore. The schools are progressive and receive good marks from parents and students alike. Most important to this book is the fact that every school has a certificated library media specialist. Roseann Fisher is the supervisor of library media services and has been instrumental in updating the library media program in Washington County. Its most recent document is titled *Washington County Library Media Essential Curriculum* and is intended to "complement and support the total instructional effort of the school" (Washington County Public Schools 1994). The library media personnel have developed a scope and sequence draft document and have fashioned it in several ways—as a chart that shows each skill and the grade level for Introduction, Achievement, and Mastery, and as a grade-by-grade instrument that shows each of the outcomes and indicators for student achievement. Washington County has used the Maryland State Department of Education *Library Media Program: A Maryland Curricular Framework* as the basis for its document. A sample of the grade by grade portion is shown on pages 63–69.

# GRADE 9

(I = Introduction A = Achievement M = Mastery)

**Outcome**—Students Will Use the Library Media Center to Locate Materials and Hardware

    **Indicator**—The student will identify the library media specialist and recognize his/her role in learning

    The student will seek help/advice of the library media specialist as:

| | |
|---|---|
| M | teacher |
| M | information specialist |
| M | media consultant |
| M | library administrator |
| M | hardware technician |
| M | production consultant |

    **Indicator**—The student will follow the policies and procedures of the library media center

    The student will identify:

| | |
|---|---|
| M | library media center services |
| M | hours of service |
| M | policies and procedures for use of facility circulation procedures |
| M | check out |
| M | return |

    **Indicator**—The student will describe the physical arrangement of the library media center

    The student will locate:

| | |
|---|---|
| M | library media center |
| M | fiction section |
| M | nonfiction section |
| M | reference section |
| M | periodicals |
| M | library catalog |
| M | biography section |
| M | audiovisual hardware and software |
| M | computer/multimedia hardware and software |
| M | vertical file |
| M | periodical indexes |
| M | circulation desk |

**Indicator**—The student will use system of classification and organization to locate materials

The student will:

| | |
|---|---|
| M | Recognize that the collection has a specific order |
| | Explain arrangement of |
| M |     fiction section |
| M |     nonfiction section |
| M |     biography section |
| M | Recognize use of alphabetical order |
| | Recognize Dewey Decimal Classification System |
| M |     identify 10 main classifications |
| M |     recognize that main classifications can be divided and subdivided into more specific subjects |
| M | Recognize that other classification systems exist |

**Indicator**—The student will identify the library media center catalog and recognize its role in learning

The student will:

| | |
|---|---|
| M | Recognize that the library catalog is an index to the library media center |
| M | Identify its organization |
| M | Apply search strategies |
| M | Differentiate between author, title and subject entries |
| | Locate information in library catalog entries |
| M |     author |
| M |     title |
| M |     subject |
| M |     call number |
| M |     illustrator |
| M |     copyright date |
| M |     publisher |
| M |     producer |
| M |     annotation |
| M |     place of publication |
| A |     editor/compiler |
| M | Use cross references |
| M | Recognize the relationship between the call number and the physical arrangement of the library media center |

**Indicator**—Demonstrate appropriate care and operation of materials and hardware

The student will:

| | |
|---|---|
| M | Demonstrate care for print materials |
| M | Demonstrate care for software |
| M | Demonstrate care for hardware |
| M | Seek assistance as needed to operate hardware |

**Outcome**—Students Will Review, Evaluate, and Select Media for an Identified Information Need

**Indicator**—The student will identify the characteristics of various media

The student will:

| | |
|---|---|
| M | Distinguish between fiction and nonfiction |
| M | Recognize types of fiction and nonfiction |
| M | Identify characteristics of print materials |
| | Identify and explain the function of book parts |
| M | cover |
| M | spine |
| M | author |
| M | title |
| M | title page |
| M | illustrator |
| M | story/text |
| M | table of contents |
| M | copyright date |
| M | publisher |
| M | glossary |
| M | index |
| M | appendix |
| M | bibliography |
| M | preface/introduction |
| M | acknowledgments/dedications |
| M | list of illustrations |
| M | Identify characteristics of audiovisual media |
| M | Identify characteristics of computer/multimedia software |
| M | Distinguish between abridged and unabridged dictionary |
| M | Distinguish between general and special dictionary |
| M | Distinguish between dictionary and general encyclopedia |
| M | Distinguish between general and special encyclopedia |
| M | Identify sources of current information |
| M | Recognize similarities and differences among magazines |
| M | Recognize similarities and differences among newspapers |

**Indicator**—The student will identify and analyze purpose for selecting media

The student will:

| | |
|---|---|
| M | State purpose of media search |
| M | Determine media characteristics appropriate for purpose |
| M | Develop search strategy |

**Indicator**—The student will develop and use criteria to select media for an identified information need

The student will:

Select media based on characteristics appropriate for
 purpose

| | |
|---|---|
| M | appeal |
| M | format |
| M | information on cover |
| M | specific title or author |
| M | illustrator |
| M | author, subject, title information in library catalog |
| M | Dewey Decimal Classification |
| M | series |
| M | length |
| M | availability |
| M | timeliness |
| M | level of difficulty |
| M | amount of information needed |
| M | content |
| M | special features |

Choose media based on recommendations from

| | |
|---|---|
| M | individuals |
| M | bibliographies and/or selection tools |
| M | Seek more than one source |
| M | Distinguish between fact and opinion |

**Outcome**—Students Will Apply Reference and Comprehension Skills to Acquire Desired Information from Various Types of Media

**Indicator**—Students will apply reference skills to locate information in a variety of sources

The student will:

| | |
|---|---|
| M | Use appropriate book parts to locate information |
| | Gain information from dictionaries |
| M | use alphabetical order to locate entry |
| M | use guide words and/or letters to locate entry |
| | interpret information in entries using |
| M | definition |
| M | pronunciation |

|   | interpret information in advanced dictionaries |
|---|---|
| M | collegiate |
| M | unabridged |
| M | subject |
| M | biographical |
| M | geographical |
|   | Gain information from encyclopedias |
| M | use alphabetical order to locate appropriate volume |
| M | use alphabetical order to locate topic in appropriate volume |
| M | use guide words to locate topic in appropriate volume |
| M | use headings and subheadings |
| M | use illustrative material |
| M | use cross references |
| M | use index |
| M | identify authors of signed articles |
| M | interpret information in special encyclopedias |
|   | Gain information from periodicals |
| M | locate and identify name of publication |
| M | locate and identify date and/or place of publication |
| M | use table of contents and/or index |
| M | locate and identify title and author of article |
| M | Gain information from almanacs |
| M | Gain information from atlases |
| M | Gain information from a thesaurus |
| M | Gain information from biographical references |
| I | Gain information from periodical indexes |
| M | Gain information from vertical file |

**Indicator**—The student will access, retrieve, and manage electronic information

The student will:

|   | Gain information from computer/multimedia sources |
|---|---|
| A | access help screen |
| A | use appropriate search strategies |
| A | use features unique to the software |
| A | recognize print capabilities |
|   | Gain information from online sources |
| A | follow library media center procedures for online use |
| A | use appropriate search strategies |
| A | recognize possible costs |

**Indicator**—The student will apply comprehension skills to acquire information from a variety of sources

The student will:

|   | Use information from |
|---|---|
| M | fiction books |
| M | nonfiction books |
| M | nonbook media |

**Outcome**—The Student Will Create Print and/or Nonprint Media

**Indicator**—The student will produce media appropriate for a particular purpose

The student will:

|   | Choose media based on |
|---|---|
| M | need and level of expertise |
| M | parameters of assignment |
| M | audience |
| M | available facilities |
| M | available hardware |
| M | available materials |
| M | cost restrictions |
| M | copyright restrictions |
| M | Follow process appropriate for chosen media |

**Outcome**—Students Will Appreciate Books and Other Media As Sources of Information and Recreation

**Indicator**—The student will use books and other media from a variety of sources to meet academic needs

The student will:

| M | Use the library media center |
|---|---|
| M | Identify location of nearest public library or bookmobile stop |
| M | Seek information outside the library media center |
| M | Develop a personal library |

**Indicator**—The student will use books and other media of more than one type

The student will:

| M | Use more than one literature form |
|---|---|
| M | Explore a variety of genre |
| M | Explore multiple themes |

**Indicator**—The student will share and promote books and other media as sources of information and recreation

The student will:

M     Share books and other media

M     Suggest materials to be considered for purchase

**Indicator**—The student will respect the rights of creators, publishers, and distributors of books and other media

The student will:

M     Avoid plagiarism when gathering information

M     Obey copyright laws relating to reproducing and utilizing media

**Indicator**—The student will respect the principles of intellectual freedom

The student will:

M     Recognize the right to have and express diverse opinions

M     Recognize that the library media center provides access to resources and resource services that express diverse opinions (Washington County Public Schools 1994)

---

It should be noted that mastery of each indicator will have been accomplished by grade 11. As this scope and sequence stands, only periodical indexes need to be introduced in grade 9, and additional work is needed to accomplish mastery in order for the student to access, retrieve, and manage electronic information. The *Washington County Library Media Essential Curriculum* states: "The library media specialist plays an important role . . . in the development of life long learning skills by providing the student with opportunities to: '

- develop computer skills and knowledge.
- make informed choices when selecting media.
- transfer search strategies learned in the library media center to real life situations.
- develop a positive attitude toward use of all libraries.
- assimilate and appreciate the concept of intellectual freedom" (Washington County Public Schools 1994).

The scope and sequence of skills and/or attitudes lets the teacher and the library media specialist see exactly what the student should have achieved at the beginning of each grade level. There is always the need for assessment and a brief review as skills are reintroduced for a specific purpose. New materials and new technologies require an introduction and practice period. New curriculum from other subject areas requires an examination of the scope and sequence to establish where the best matches can occur within the library media program.

School library media programs are implemented in various ways, and there is no right way. District-level leadership is essential in selling the selected program to the district's school administrators and the board of education. Most important, perhaps, is assuring that all school library media specialists understand and adopt the program as their own. Library media personnel who are new to the system must have the benefit of a thorough orientation to the district's library media program; also, it is helpful for the supervisor to have a brief session with all teachers who are new to the system. Then expectations and delivery of library media programs coincide.

# Chapter 7

## The English Curriculum— District and State

Almost every state has developed a core curriculum for the study of English-language arts for the secondary school; Maryland is no exception. The Maryland State Department of Education (MSDE) has put into place a program for schools within the state called the Maryland School Performance Program. Core curriculum has been developed for each subject area, and this curriculum is interpreted in the districts as essential curriculum, meaning the goals written in the state documents must be addressed in classrooms across the state. But there is ample room for the district and/or the school to develop goals pertaining to their specific needs as well. At the present time, an assessment program (Maryland School Performance Assessment Program, or MSPAP) is in place for grades 3, 5, and 8. All students in these grades are tested in mathematics, social studies, science, and English-language arts, including reading and writing. The purpose of these tests is to hold the schools accountable for students' learning, and the individual school has the responsibility for the assessment results. This assessment program is expected to include grade 11 in the early 2000s: therefore, the core curricula are in place for the senior high school as a major part of the School Performance Program.[1] It should be noted that the core curricula documents from the state are developed with majority input from teachers and supervisors from the districts.

Since the subject of this chapter is the English curriculum, we will look at the *High School Core Learning Goals for the English Program* as developed for the MSPAP. The content team that wrote the program consisted of district English supervisors, English teachers, college instructors, state department personnel, a school administrator, and a library media specialist. In the introductory piece of *High School Core Learning Goals for English* (see pp. 72-73), the rationale for teaching English is given.

# High School Core Learning Goals for English

What is English? How should it be taught and assessed?

The purpose of high school English is to provide experiences that foster thoughtful, fluent, and responsible use of language of the sort required by informed citizens to reach carefully reasoned decisions and express their views effectively. High school English courses build upon literacy skills learned in families and communities, in elementary school, and throughout the middle learning years. Reading, writing, speaking, and listening comprise the processes of English while language and literature comprise the content. English is composed of those processes and content areas relevant to successful living which are integral to the ability to express, create, learn, interpret, and stimulate thoughts and feelings. To be learned and used effectively, the processes of reading, writing, speaking, and listening, and the content of language and literature, are best taught in an integrated manner and assessed in the same way.

Reading, writing, speaking, and listening require the learner to engage in preparatory activities and then to construct meaning, compose, and evaluate. When constructing meaning through reading, listening, or viewing, the learner is involved in acquiring information, organizing ideas, appreciating the art of literature, and integrating new learning with previous knowledge. When composing, the learner generates ideas, reviews, makes adjustments, revises, and considers changes based on established and evolving criteria. When evaluating, the learner develops an understanding of the purposefulness underlying the intent, his/her own or someone else's, while also developing criteria for judging effectiveness of the communication involved. Finally, the learner must be able to employ, when appropriate, those criteria in his or her own work by applying conventions of standard written and spoken English.

In the English classroom, students interpret, generate, and evaluate texts. "Text" is used to mean all author-created materials, in both print and nonprint media. Students entering the 21st century need to be discriminating users of text wherever it occurs: classic and contemporary literature, multi-cultural literature, information obtained from online sources and computer software, student-created writings, speeches, films, plays, and other formal and informal performances and exhibits involving language and creative expression.

Students must also be able to retrieve information from both traditional and technological sources and to express themselves, orally and in writing, in effective ways which can be understood by a variety of audiences. The need for information retrieval, effective communication, and discriminating use of text is not confined to the English classroom. English teachers share responsibility for teaching those skills and processes with all teachers of all content areas that require their use.

Students should be able to apply the communication processes effectively and to assume conscious control of their language and interaction with texts. The study of language enhances the study of literature and the effectiveness of the learner's oral and written communication. Language is learned best in pursuit of genuine ends and purposes. Thus, grammar and mechanics are learned and assessed most effectively in the context of a student's reading, writing, speaking, and listening.

Language and literature comprise the content and frame the processes in the English classroom. A careful balance in instruction ensures that both content and processes are truly integrated and all receive appropriate emphasis. Student assessment requires the same careful balance. The current dialogue toward the development of national standards for English reflects the integration of content and process within content. The content goals for English, when integrated with the goals of *Skills for Success*,[2] provide for enriched learning, the development of lifelong skills, and the fostering of capable, productive decision makers.

Literature is of particular importance in the high school English classroom. The study of English in a literature-based program encourages learners to understand, appreciate, and enjoy their world. As students study literature, their experiences and backgrounds influence their understanding of the text while their understanding of their own experiences is sharpened and enlarged.

Works for study in the English classroom should be of significant merit, reflect many literary traditions, and should be drawn from diverse writing styles and points of view that reflect the concerns of both genders and a wide range of races and cultures. Traditional works that have a history of study serve as bridges to other times and between readers of different generations (MSDE 1996, 1–2).

---

The document, shown here on pages 74-82, is arranged with a goal as the heading, followed by a brief explanation to ascertain implementation, several expectations which include indicators of learning, and sample instructional activities. For the purpose of this book, only selected instructional activities will be used. There are a total of four goals. Sample instructional activities are given for each Expectation in part B. Since sample activities are used in one of the district documents addressed later in this chapter, this part of the state Core Learning Goals will be used sparingly.

# Goals and Expectations

## GOAL 1
The student will demonstrate the ability to respond to a
text by employing personal experiences and critical analysis.

The following key ideas merit elaboration and further explanation if a teacher is to implement this Core Learning Goal successfully.

Each expectation focuses on a different aspect of the word "respond." Expectation 1 emphasizes the behaviors associated with strategic readers. Expectation 2 targets the relationship between literary elements and textual interpretations. Expectation 3 stresses the independent interpretation and critical analysis of literature, films, videos, oral interpretations, and theatrical performances.

As defined by the indicators, "literature" includes traditional print materials (poems, short stories, essays, novels, and plays) and nonprint materials (films and "live" performances). The same careful strategies that are taught and applied to one should be applied to the other. Although reading, viewing, and listening are not the same, they are all complementary "receptive" processes that are mutually informing.

Developmental psychology has shown that a personal response is inevitably the initial response. For that reason, personal responses are the best starting point for leading students eventually to a full critical analysis of literature. Similarly, helping students to apply the indicators to literature they have selected is as significant as enabling them to interpret teacher-selected works.

**1. EXPECTATION:** The student will use effective strategies before, during, and after reading, viewing, and listening to self-selected and assigned materials.

    A.   Indicators of Learning

        (1)   The student will use pre-reading strategies appropriate to both the text and purpose for reading by surveying the text, accessing prior knowledge, formulating questions, setting purpose(s), and making predictions.

        (2)   The student will use during-reading strategies appropriate to both the text and purpose for reading by visualizing, making connections, and using fix-up strategies such as rereading, questioning, and summarizing.

        (3)   The student will use after-reading strategies appropriate to both the text and purpose for reading by summarizing, comparing, contrasting, synthesizing, drawing conclusions, and validating the purpose for reading.

(4)  The student will apply before, during, and after reading strategies when responding to nonprint text, e.g., film, speakers, theatre, performance, audio texts, and interactive media.

(5)  The student will identify specific structural elements of particular literary forms: poetry, short story, novel, drama, essay, biography, autobiography, journalistic writing, and film.

2. **EXPECTATION:** The student will construct, examine, and extend meaning of traditional and contemporary works recognized as having significant literary merit.

A.  Indicators of Learning

(1)  The student will consider the contributions of plot, character, setting, conflict, and point of view when constructing the meaning of a text.

(2)  The student will examine meaning by determining how the speaker, organization, sentence structure, word choice, tone, rhythm, and imagery reveal an author's purpose.

(3)  The student will explain the effectiveness of stylistic elements such as syntax, rhetorical devices, and choice of details which communicate an author's purpose.

(4)  The student will explain connections between and among themes and styles of two or more texts.

(5)  The student will extend or further develop meaning by explaining the implications of the text for the reader or contemporary society.

(6)  The student will extend or further develop meaning by comparing texts presented in different media.

B.  Sample Instructional Activity

The student will read Shakespeare's play and view Zefferelli's film *Romeo and Juliet*. The student will examine the consequences of the major characters' actions, including how those actions shape the perceptions of the other characters toward that character. The student will discuss how differences between the film and the play affect audience perceptions of the characters; for example, how the omission of the death of Paris in the film affects our perception of Romeo.

**3. EXPECTATION:** The student will explain and give evidence to support perceptions about print and nonprint works.

    A.   Indicators of Learning

        (1)   The student will explain how language and textual devices create meaning.

        (2)   The student will interpret a work by using a critical approach (e.g., reader response, historical, cultural, biographical, structural) that is supported with textual references.

        (3)   The student will identify features of language that create voice and tone.

        (4)   The student will explain how devices such as staging, lighting, blocking, special effects, graphics, and other techniques unique to a nonprint medium are used to create meaning and evoke response.

        (5)   The student will explain how common and universal experiences serve as the source of literary themes which cross time and cultures.

        (6)   The student will assess the literary merit of a text.

# GOAL 2

The student will demonstrate the ability to compose in a variety of modes by developing content, employing specific forms, and selecting language appropriate for a particular audience and purpose.

The word "compose" has been chosen deliberately because it embraces oral, written, and visual communication and facilitates an instructional emphasis on the common principles of communicating—either separately or in combination—via speech, writing, computer graphics, and video production. The term "compose" also alludes to the writing process, an instructional model in use within Maryland schools for more than a decade. Furthermore, "composing" has natural applicability to such technologically essential skills as word processing and desktop publishing and describes more precisely than does the term "writing" what it is that students actually do when using a word processor.

The term "mode" refers to rhetorical modes such as descriptions, narration, exposition, and argumentation. Specific prose and poetic forms include but are not limited to dialogue, letter, essay, couplet, quatrain, and free verse. Language choices are considered "appropriate" if they match the communicative context (i.e., the audience, topic, and purpose) of a given oral or written communication task.

**1. EXPECTATION:** The student will compose oral, written, and visual presentations which inform, persuade, and express personal ideas.

    A.   Indicators of Learning

        (1)   The student will compose to inform by using appropriate types of prose (e.g., to explain a process, to discuss cause and effect).

        (2)   The student will compose to describe, using prose and/or poetic forms.

        (3)   The student will compose to express personal ideas, using prose and/or poetic forms.

        (4)   The student will compose persuasive texts that support, modify, or refute a position and include effective rhetorical strategies.

    B.   Sample Instructional Activity

The student will use previously learned nonprint devices and conventions to create a videotape, slide show, or multi-media presentation that informs a designated audience about an issue or topic.

**2. EXPECTATION:** The student will compose texts using the prewriting, drafting, and revision strategies of effective writers and speakers.

    A.   Indicators of Learning

        (1)   The student will use a variety of prewriting strategies to generate and develop ideas.

        (2)   The student will select and organize ideas for specific audiences and purposes.

        (3)   The student will revise texts for clarity, completeness and effectiveness.

        (4)   The student will rehearse oral texts for effective application of diction, intonation, and rhetorical strategies, such as introductions, sequence, illustrations, and conclusions.

        (5)   The student will use suitable traditional and electronic resources to refine presentations and edit texts for effective and appropriate use of language and conventions, such as capitalization, punctuation, spelling, and pronunciation.

        (6)   The student will prepare the final product for presentation to an audience.

**3. EXPECTATION:** The student will locate, retrieve, and use information from various sources to accomplish a purpose.

    A.   Indicators of Learning

        (1)   The student will identify sources of information on a self-selected or given topic.

        (2)   The student will use various information retrieval sources (traditional and electronic) to obtain information on a self-selected and/or given topic. Electronic sources include automated catalogs, CD-ROM products, and on-line services like Internet, World Wide Web, and others.

        (3)   The student will use a systematic process for recording, documenting, and organizing information.

        (4)   The student will take a position and support it with documented information from an authoritative source.

        (5)   The student will synthesize information from two or more sources to fulfill a self-selected or given purpose.

---

# GOAL 3

The student will demonstrate the ability to control language by applying the conventions of standard English in writing and speaking.

---

The ability to control language is contained in all of the English Core Learning Goals since language is one of the two content areas of a strong English curriculum. Language ability is important enough to focus on as a separate goal in addition to addressing it in other goals.

Controlling language refers to the ability to make language choices that enhance the impression of the speaker or writer as well as enhance the credibility of the message. "Control" subsumes such behavior as choosing, selecting, and manipulating language so that it is appropriate to an audience, occasion, and purpose.

"Standard English" is a convenient term used to refer to the "language of employability," that variety of spoken and written English on which employers often base hiring and promotion decisions.

**1. EXPECTATION:** The student will demonstrate understanding of the nature and structure of language, including grammar concepts and skills, to strengthen control of oral and written language.

    A.   Indicators of Learning

        (1)   The student will determine the advantages and limitations of speech and writing when communicating in various situations for specific audiences and purposes.

(2)  The student will describe how intonation, pitch, volume, pause, and rate all influence meaning.

(3)  The student will explain how words are classified grammatically by meaning, position, form, and function.

(4)  The student will differentiate grammatically complete sentences from non-sentences.

(5)  The student will incorporate subjects, predicates, and modifiers when composing original sentences.

(6)  The student will compound various sentence elements—subjects, predicates, modifiers, phrases, and clauses—to link or contrast related ideas.

(7)  The student will vary sentence types—simple, complex, compound, and compound/complex—to sustain reader or listener interest.

(8)  The student will expand sentences by positioning clauses and phrases to function as nouns, adjectives, or adverbs.

(9)  The student will recognize, combine, and transform basic sentence patterns to vary sentence structure, to emphasize selected ideas, and to achieve syntactic maturity.

2. **EXPECTATION:** The student will identify how language choices in writing and speaking affect thoughts and feelings.

   A.  Indicators of Learning

   (1)  The student will choose a level of language, formal to informal, appropriate for a specific audience, situation, or purpose.

   (2)  The student will differentiate connotative from denotative meanings of words.

   (3)  The student will describe how readers or listeners might respond differently to the same words.

   (4)  The student will describe regional and social language differences.

   (5)  The student will describe the impact of regional and social variations of language on listener or reader response.

B.  Sample Instructional Activity

>   After reading and discussing the poem, "We Real Cool," by Gwendolyn Brooks, the student will identify the speaker of the poem and support that identification through language examples. Then the student will identify possible audiences for whom the poem might have been intended and support the identification through language examples. Finally, the student will convert the thought of the poem for a specific audience and explain language choices made for that audience.

**3. EXPECTATION:** The student will use capitalization, punctuation, and correct spelling appropriately.

A.  Indicators of Learning

(1)  The student will edit texts for spelling, capitalization, and punctuation using available resources.

(2)  The student will use available resources to correct or confirm editorial choices.

---

# GOAL 4
The student will demonstrate the ability to evaluate the content, organization, and language of texts.

---

This goal is designed to help students integrate the knowledge and skills inherent in the first three goals and apply them to their own reading and writing. The enjoyment of literature is enhanced by the ability to evaluate how the author created the text. In the same way, the pleasure of creating texts is deepened by the ability to analyze their effectiveness for different audiences and different purposes.

**1. EXPECTATION:** The student will describe the effect that a given text, heard or read, has on a listener or reader.

A.  Indicators of Learning

(1)  The student will state and explain a personal response to a given text.

(2)  The student will identify specific words, phrases, scenes, images, and symbols that support a personal response to a given text.

**2. EXPECTATION:** The student will assess the effectiveness of choice of details, organizational pattern, word choice, syntax, use of figurative language, and rhetorical devices in the student's own composing.

    A.   Indicators of Learning

        (1)   The student will assess the effectiveness of diction that reveals his or her purpose.

        (2)   The student will explain how the specific language and expression used by the writer or speaker affects reader or listener response.

        (3)   The student will evaluate the use of transitions and their effectiveness in a text.

        (4)   The student will explain how repetition of words, phrases, structural features, and ideas affect the meaning and/or tone of a text.

    B.   Sample Instructional Activity

        The student will read Mark Twain's "A Double-Barreled Detective Story," a writing which uses a series of exaggerated descriptions to lull the reader into a false sense of beauty and tranquillity. After reading the passage containing those descriptions, the student will respond to questions such as the following:

        •  What is the mood?

        •  What emotion(s) dominate?

        •  Create a pictograph of the passage.

        The student will then use a dictionary to define all unfamiliar words in the passage and return to the questions above, this time concentrating on contradictions of place, time, and mood. Finally, the student will explain which features of the writing have given two different interpretations of the passage.

**3. EXPECTATION:** The student will evaluate textual changes in a work and explain how these changes alter tone, clarify meaning, address a particular audience, or fulfill a purpose.

    A.   Indicators of Learning

        (1)   The student will alter the tone of his or her text by revising its diction.

(2)　The student will justify revisions in syntax and diction from a previous draft of his or her same text by explaining how the change affects meaning.

(3)　The student will alter his or her text to present the same content to a different audience via the same or different media.

(4)　The student will compare the difference in effect of two texts on a given subject (MSDE 1996).

*High School Core Learning Goals for the English Program* reprinted with permission of the Maryland State Department of Education.

After the core curriculum has been decided upon and printed, the committee responsible for its development works with state department personnel to deliver the information via professional meetings to every English-language arts supervisor in each of the districts. Often, the supervisors who have served on the Core Curriculum committee take the information back to their districts and form committees to begin to align their curriculum with the state goals. The English supervisors provide inservice sessions to the English chairpersons and teachers in their districts as new requirements are introduced. Needless to say, the manner in which the core or essential curriculum is developed and delivered will vary from district to district—depending upon district needs, resources, and leadership. Almost always, the model that is used is one that allows for field-testing the recommended curriculum—usually for a year—and having the teachers and students provide feedback. It is then revised, and the best resources to use in implementing it are ascertained. Local boards of education approve curriculum; parent and community groups need to be informed of new curricular developments, and school library media personnel must be alerted when changes are made that affect purchases and use of library resources. If library media specialists are included in the development of curriculum, this step is almost automatic. If not, the English supervisor has the responsibility to assure that the needed resources will be requested through the library media program.

##  Howard County's English Curriculum— Grade 9

The document *The Essential Curriculum Documents: English 8–9*, a portion of which is reproduced on pages 83–90, was developed in the summer of 1997 by a curriculum committee from the Howard County Public Schools in Maryland. One of the English supervisors, Allan Starkey, also served on the state's Core Curriculum committee.

# English 9—Essential Curriculum

Howard County essential curriculum documents identify what students should know and be able to do in each subject they study. As such, they represent the "non-negotiables" of instruction. Quarterly assessments are under development to help teachers with determining how successful students have been with accomplishing the stated instructional goals and objectives. These assessments, to be field tested and revised during the current school year, will be published with future editions of the essential English curriculum.

The essential curriculum for English 9 consists of the three traditional components of literature, language, and composition with goals and objectives stated for each. Literature and composition goals have been combined and listed by unit title to show the integration that characterizes sound instruction in the English language arts. Immediately following them, related language objectives have been listed separately so that teachers can more easily determine the language goals and objectives to target for intensive study. Where appropriate, however, language objectives have also been inserted under those goals for which they seem most related, to guide teachers' decisions about how best to integrate grammar skills with literature study and written composition.

Essential goals and objectives from the 8th grade essential curriculum have also been printed here to help teachers know the understandings and skills on which they may build and also to facilitate decision making about review or remediation when necessary. Differentiation for gifted and talented students is indicated through a tiered approach. Those objectives to be emphasized in gifted and talented classes are the final objectives under each goal and are coded with a G/T placed in parenthesis after the objective.

Composition goals for each grade have been classified into four categories: Exposition, Persuasion, Prose and Dramatic Narratives, and Poetry. The category of each composition goal is indicated parenthetically immediately following the goal statement. Since research into composition instruction confirms that the most effective curriculums provide students with a variety of writing experiences, students must write regularly in various forms and modes. Composition goals throughout the essential English curriculum aim to provide students with this desired variety and balance. Whenever possible, goals have been conceived and stated in such a way that an oral composition activity may be substituted for writing. This will provide teachers with opportunities to let students practice important speaking skills within the context of the regular English program.

The curriculum committee has revised related language skills only slightly to make them more specific in places and also to include an explicit reference to the traditional sentence types, a request we received from many teachers. The following six categories have been retained although not all occur on each grade level: Sentence Elements, Sentences and Non-sentences, Modifiers, Usage and Agreement, Style, and Mechanics. Many of the decisions about the grammar sequence were based on the research about grammar instruction and accompanying instructional approaches described by Rei R. Noguchi in *Grammar and the Teaching of Writing*, available from the National Council of Teachers of English. Reference copies are available in each school.

The language arts staff hopes the essential curriculum documents help English teachers make efficient and effective instructional decisions.

[The first two units will be presented in their entirety; the final two units will include goals only.][3]

# English 9—Essential Curriculum

## Literature and Composition

### Unit I: Writers Record Experiences

**Goal 1.** The student will demonstrate the ability to understand how a writer's language reflects his or her life experiences and projects a personal voice.

**Objectives**—The student will demonstrate the ability to:

  a.  Use effective before, during, and after reading strategies with each selection.

  b.  Identify the forms of personal narrative as interior monologue, dramatic monologue, soliloquy, dialogue, correspondence, journal, autobiography, or memoir.

  c.  Identify passages which evoke a personal voice and reveal the physical, mental, or emotional stance from which a speaker observes a subject.

  d.  Identify and explain how an author's use of figurative devices affects meaning in a narrative text.

  e.  Evaluate the effect of sentences and nonsentences in relation to a writer's purpose.

  f.  Explain how choice of paragraphing, sequencing, and language may accomplish a writer's purpose and affect reader response. (G/T)

**Goal 2.** The student will demonstrate the ability to read selected narratives and identify common, shared human experiences.

**Objectives**—Students will demonstrate the ability to:

  a.  Differentiate between fact and fiction in personal narratives.

  b.  Locate and identify passages which reveal regionalism and local color in short stories.

    c.   Identify main idea or theme in narrative poems and monologues.

    d.   Compare their personal experiences with those encountered while reading various authors.

    e.   Describe themes of personal narratives, including but not limited to the following: birth, the search for identity, coming to terms with sexuality, intellectual growth, social adjustment, career development, and mortality.

    f.   Use textual evidence to defend an oral or written interpretation of literature.

    g.   Identify factors that contribute to creating a writer's unique voice.(G/T)

**Goal 3.**    The student will demonstrate the ability to complete a diagnostic writing sample that confirms current levels of achievement in both grammar and written composition. (Exposition)

**Objectives**—The student will demonstrate the ability to:

    a.   Determine through class discussion the values of maintaining a writing portfolio.

    b.   Summarize past experiences with writing both in and out of school, and describe current attitudes, strengths, and goals.

    c.   Develop a paragraph that assesses one's current status as a writer and includes the following:

- a focused topic sentence;
- a minimum of three supporting sentences arranged in some logical order; and
- a concluding sentence that clinches some idea about the student as a writer.

    d.   Revise the paragraph based on questions and comments from peers.

    e.   Edit the writing to confirm mastery of K-8 grammar, usage, and mechanical skills.

    f.   Develop cooperatively a scoring rubric for use as a teacher, peer, or self-assessment tool.

g.  Establish a writing portfolio to be used later in the course as the basis for

- practicing revision skills
- writing reflection pieces
- assembling a presentation portfolio

h.  Develop a multi-paragraph "writing autobiography" which traces one's development as a writer over several years of schooling. (G/T)

**Goal 4.**  The student will demonstrate the ability to develop an autobiographical incident or series of related incidents into a personal narrative or memoir. (Prose and Dramatic Narratives)

**Objectives**—The student will demonstrate the ability to:

a.  Recall and develop one or more memorable incidents through freewriting, listing, or webbing.

b.  Identify a specific focus, audience, and purpose.

c.  Include concrete, sensory details to make the incidents distinct for readers.

d.  Arrange details chronologically.

e.  Vary use of simple, compound, complex, and compound-complex sentences.

f.  Compose sentences using semicolons in place of coordinating conjunctions.

g.  Revise using computer technology.

h.  Include an introduction that indicates a particular attitude toward the experiences being conveyed. (G/T)

i.  Use both denotative and connotative diction as well as figurative language to convey a predetermined voice and tone. (G/T)

## Unit II: Writers Invent Character and Point of View

**Goal 1.**  The student will demonstrate the ability to read selected poetry, short stories, novels, and plays to determine how character development affects meaning.

**Objectives**—The student will demonstrate the ability to:

a.  Apply strategic reading skills to each assigned reading.

    b.   Explain how character is revealed by

- what an author says
- what a character says or does
- what other characters say about him or her
- what the character thinks

    c.   Describe the correlations between a character's personality and physical appearance.

    d.   Identify the descriptive words and phrases that a writer uses to illustrate a particular character or characteristic.

    e.   Identify specific passages in which an author develops a character directly and indirectly.

    f.   Explain why stereotyping is used by writers and how it may be interpreted by readers.

    g.   Distinguish various types of characters: static, dynamic, flat, and round.

    h.   Compose an original interior or dramatic monologue from the perspective of a literary character. (G/T)

**Goal 2.**   The student will demonstrate the ability to read selected poetry, short stories, novels, and plays to determine how point of view affects meaning.

**Objectives**—The student will demonstrate the ability to:

    a.   Identify the narrative point of view in a given work as either first person subjective, first person limited, third person limited, third person omniscient, or third person objective.

    b.   Identify specific narrative passages that are subjective and objective.

    c.   Identify diction used to establish a particular locale in any time period.

    d.   Describe the role or the influence of the narrator within a given work.

    e.   Explain how point of view limits or enhances the narrator's ability to reveal what characters do, think, and feel.

    f.   Explain how the narrator's point of view influences the intimacy or connection of the reader to the characters and the story as a whole.

g. Explain how a reader's impression of the characters in a work is affected by how the narrator chooses to describe them.

h. Rewrite a description of a place from another point of view.

i. Distinguish between point of view as a literary technique and point of view as one's opinion.

j. Distinguish between the narrative technique and the author's opinion. (G/T)

**Goal 3.** The student will demonstrate the ability to write a description of a place, real or imagined, aiming for a dominant impression. (Prose and Dramatic Narratives)

**Objectives**—The student will demonstrate the ability to:

a. Create a topic sentence that indicates the setting and the writer's relationship to it.

b. Include concrete sensory details which make the locale and time period distinct for readers.

c. Arrange details in spatial order from left to right, top to bottom, near to far, or most prominent to least prominent.

d. Compose sentences using modifiers in a variety of sentence positions.

e. Write a conclusion which restates the dominant impression.

f. Use semicolons in place of coordinating conjunctions to link independent clauses.

g. Observe the conventions of standard edited English when preparing the final draft.

h. Write a reflection on the process used to compose this description of a place, to be included in the student's journal or portfolio.

i. Convey a particular attitude towards the subject through consistent use of well-chosen details. (G/T)

**Goal 4.** The student will demonstrate the ability to write a description of a character in action. (Prose and Dramatic Narratives)

**Objectives**—The student will demonstrate the ability to:

a. Select a real-life individual to use as the subject.

b.  Write an introduction that indicates a setting and the subject's relationship to it.

c.  Reveal character traits primarily through what the subject does or says.

- Use strong action words throughout.
- Include dialogue that reveals personality traits.

d.  Include descriptive words or phrases to convey unique physical traits and to create a distinct locale.

e.  Compose sentences using modifiers in a variety of sentence positions.

f.  Write a conclusion which captures an impression of the total character.

g.  Observe the conventions of standard edited English when preparing the final draft.

h.  Write a reflection on the process used to compose this character sketch, to be included in the students journal or portfolio.

i.  Eliminate details which do not contribute to a central or dominant character trait. (G/T)

j.  Vary sentence openers, patterns, types, and lengths. (G/T)

## Unit III: Writers Choose Language: Literary and Persuasive

**Goal 1.**  The student will demonstrate the ability to analyze and imitate the literary techniques that writers use for various purposes.

**Goal 2.**  The student will demonstrate the ability to understand how persuasive language is based on emotional appeals and propaganda devices.

**Goal 3.**  The student will demonstrate the ability to create an original poem that conveys an emotion. (Poetry)

## Unit IV: Writers Create Meaning: Theme and Variation

**Goal 1.**  The student will demonstrate the ability to identify the theme of a selection as it emerges within conflict, plot, character, setting, point of view, tone, and poetic language.

**Goal 2.**  The student will demonstrate the ability to state a theme and explain how it unifies the elements within a work. (Exposition)

**Goal 3.** The student will demonstrate the ability to compose a persuasive essay or debate a controversial idea derived from interpreting several pieces of literature, music, or art. (Persuasion)

**Goal 4.** The student will demonstrate the ability to use his or her portfolio to assess personal growth in written composition for the semester or year (Exposition) (Howard County Public Schools 1997).

At the end of this document, there is a brief section titled "Related Language Skills" that deals with sentences and nonsentences, usage and agreement, style, and mechanics.

The Howard County curriculum embraces the state's Core Curriculum while allowing ample room for district, and ultimately school needs, resources, and teaching and learning styles. While the eighth grade English curriculum is not included in this book, it is interesting to note that it is included in the document received by teachers in Howard County. This is not a scope and sequence format, but it certainly gives the ninth grade English teacher a working knowledge of what expectations to have for those incoming high school students. Also, this document is labeled "Pilot Copy," and upon reading the introduction, the teacher knows there can and will be changes made as the goals and objectives are implemented with students.

 ## English Curriculum in Baltimore County

There are many approaches to curriculum and to the implementation of the Core Curriculum in Maryland. Baltimore County, Maryland, has taken a different way of handling the state's requirement. Many people assume that Baltimore County includes the city of Baltimore as part of its environs; this is not so. The county surrounds the city, horseshoe fashion, bordering Anne Arundel County to the south. The city is a separate entity. Many of the city's problems spill over into the county, but one can see large suburban areas and even rural acreage in various sections. Henry McGraw is the English supervisor who works almost exclusively with the high school English program and with 25 high schools, including magnet schools and academies. It is a time-consuming task. Baltimore County Public Schools has a comprehensive English-language arts curriculum in place and has taken the Core Curriculum as it was written at the state level to incorporate into the existing English course of study. The state's Core Curriculum is used as a separate document, as a result of a decision made by a curriculum committee in 1997. The primary difference one will see in the document as it appears at the state level and in the Baltimore County Public Schools is in the Sample Instructional Activity piece (see pp. 91–93). McGraw and the curriculum committee developed their own activities to demonstrate examples of how the goals, expectations, and indicators can be implemented using the resources already in place. Samples from three grade levels follow.[4]

# Indicators of Learning: English—Grades 9, 10, 11

## Grade 9

**Goal 3.** The student will demonstrate the ability to control language by applying the conventions of standard English in writing and speaking.

**Expectation 1.** The student will demonstrate understanding of the nature and structure of language, including grammar concepts and skills, to strengthen control of oral and written language.

Indicators:

- The student will explain how words are classified grammatically by meaning, position, form, and function.

- The student will differentiate grammatically complete sentences from nonsentences.

- The student will incorporate subjects, predicates, and modifiers when composing original sentences.

### Sample Instructional Activity 3.1

From forth the fatal loins of these two foes

A pair of star-crossed lovers take their life.

*(Romeo and Juliet)*, Prologue, lines 5-6.

Divide the above lines from the prologue of *Romeo and Juliet* into parts of speech (prepositional phrases, noun phrases, and verbs), color-code them, and write them on sentence strips. Have students work in groups to arrange the parts into sentences that make the most sense to them, and have groups present and justify their arrangements. Have students discuss and determine which parts of the sentence are the most moveable (prepositional phrases) and which are not (noun phrases and verbs). At this point, help students define the meaning, position, form, and function of prepositional phrases and cite several other examples of prepositions and prepositional phrases. Have students verify the correct positioning of the sentence parts by consulting the prologue of *Romeo and Juliet*. Help students define unfamiliar vocabulary words and ask them to interpret the meaning of these lines.

As a class, identify the grammatical structure of the sentence from *Romeo and Juliet*:

> prepositional phrase
>
> prepositional phrase
>
> noun phrase (composed of a modifier, noun, and prepositional phrase)
>
> verb
>
> noun phrase (functioning as a direct object)

Have students work in pairs to rewrite the prologue line in more modern language, following Shakespeare's grammatical structure.

---

# Grade 10

**Goal 2.**   The student will demonstrate the ability to compose in a variety of modes by developing content, employing specific forms, and selecting language appropriate for a particular audience and purpose.

**Expectation 3.** The student will locate, retrieve, and use information from various sources to accomplish a purpose.

Indicators:

- The student will use various information retrieval sources (traditional and electronic) to obtain information on a self-selected and/or given topic. Electronic sources include automated catalogs, CD-ROM products, and on-line services like Internet, World-Wide Web, and others.
- The student will synthesize information from two or more sources to fulfill a self-selected or given purpose.

## Sample Instructional Activity 2.3

Have students use two or more sources to research an author, a literary work, a time period, a locale, a historical event, or a current issue to prepare an oral or written report. Research should include the use of primary and secondary sources as well as traditional and electronic methods of information retrieval. Review with the class notetaking skills such as paraphrasing, outlining, summarizing, and quoting. Also review documentation forms, especially the use of parenthetical (internal) citations.

Depending on the nature of the class and the complexity of the topic, the final product may be a formal research paper, an oral presentation, an outline, a written report, a travel brochure, a biographical sketch, a newspaper article, a video report, a multi-media presentation, an editorial commentary, or a pamphlet which states a position about a controversial issue.

# Grade 11

**Goal 1:** The student will demonstrate the ability to respond to a text by employing personal experiences and critical analysis.

**Expectation 1.** The student will use effective strategies before, during, and after reading, viewing, and listening to self-selected and assigned materials.

Indicators:

- The student will identify specific structural elements of particular literary forms: poetry, short story, novel, drama, essay, biography, autobiography, journalistic writing, and film.

## Sample Instructional Activity 1.1

Before students read/listen to *The Crucible*, have students suggest examples of times when a group of people may have overreacted to a situation and made the situation seem out of control (e.g., O. J. Simpson trial, Tickle-Me-Elmo craze, Beanie Babies craze, Rodney King verdict, *War of the Worlds, Independence Day*). Differentiate between the situations which are fads and those which generate fear. Then indicate that these are examples of mass hysteria. Have the students create a definition for *mass hysteria* and explain that this is a major concept in the play by relating it to McCarthyism. Next, give students a copy of *The Crucible* to preview and have the class discuss the structure of a play to create a glossary of terms commonly associated with drama (such as stage directions, tone, mood, setting). Then have students read, view, or listen to Act I. After discussing Act I, have students predict what will happen in Act II as the level of hysteria increases. Have students write their ideas in dramatic form (Baltimore County Public Schools 1997).

---

Both Howard County Public Schools and Baltimore County Public Schools have exemplary English programs in place in their high schools. As one peruses the various samples from the foregoing curriculum documents, there are many places where library and information skills could be integrated with the English curricula. Ways in which this integration can be implemented will be specifically addressed in the next chapter.

 **Notes**

1. Additional information about Maryland's School Performance Assessment Program may be obtained from: Maryland State Department of Education, School Performance, Product and Service Development Office, 200 West Baltimore Street, Baltimore, MD 21201.

2. *Skills for Success* is a document prepared at the state level by a committee of business people, educators from all levels, tradespersons and other community members. It addresses the needs of the world into which the high school graduate will enter in very practical terms, and it is intended to be integrated into each high school curriculum document.

3. Information about Howard County Public School's curriculum may be obtained from: Howard County Public Schools, Office of English/Language Arts, 10910 Route 108, Ellicott City, MD 21042.

4. Information about the Baltimore County English curriculum may be obtained from: Office of English/Language Arts, Baltimore County Public Schools, 6901 North Charles Street, Towson, MD 21204.

# Chapter 8

## Library and Information Skills and the English Program in the School

As one looks at the many ways in which an integrated program of skills can be implemented, it is difficult to choose models that can be successful for the majority of users. But, as has been the strategy used in this book, there are several examples with which I am familiar, and the reader may take from these models what would be most useful for his or her program. Several have been designed by library media specialists and English teachers at the district level but are intended for use by all high schools within the district, and others have been developed by media specialists and English-language arts teachers for their individual schools.

## Carroll County's High School Media Curriculum

Most school districts in Maryland use the *Learning Outcomes in Library Media Skills* published by the Maryland State Department of Education as the basis for any media program development. Carroll County is no exception. This district lies to the northwest of Baltimore City and has been largely agricultural; it is the site of Western Maryland College, a small liberal arts college with a strong education department. Carroll County is changing its rural face and looks more like suburbia as ready access to Baltimore becomes more available. Irene Hildebrandt is the library media supervisor and has built upon past leadership in the county by bringing current technology into school media centers. Additionally, she facilitated the development of library media curriculum during the summer of 1997 by bringing together teachers and media specialists. At the high school level, media specialists and English teachers from Francis Scott Key High School and South Carroll High School were able to rely upon past successes to create sample lessons for the high school program. While these lessons were created at the system level, they are based upon actual practice and are intended to be adapted for use in the high school library media instructional program throughout the county. The document (in draft form) is titled *High School Library Media Curriculum.*

## Searching Techniques

The first sample lesson, shown on page 97, deals with searching techniques, a topic every high school media specialist must deal with again and again in every subject area.

# Search Strategy

Research skills instruction begins with a successful search strategy. The purpose of the search strategy is to help students determine what information they need to find as well as identify key words and potential sources of information. Strategies should be developed by the media specialist and the classroom teacher as the media lesson is being planned. The scope of the media activity will determine how extensive the search strategy will be. In some cases a quick key word review will suffice, while for some lessons a more in-depth strategy should be completed before the students come to the media center.

The most valuable part of the search strategy is the list of search or key words. Student researchers have always had a problem with key words and, with the addition of electronic databases to the variety of resources to be searched, the identification of key search words is an essential skills to be learned. A good list of key words provides the student not only with a means to access information but also a tool to use in evaluating the usefulness of the information found.

Ideally, a basic search strategy should be employed that can be used with a variety of resources. When specific resources are required for an activity, search strategies tailored to that resource should be used. For example, when introducing students to search engines on the Internet it will be necessary to do a lesson not only on key words, but also on how to conduct a Boolean search.

Included in this curriculum are examples of a basic search strategy to be used for any resource search as well as tips and strategies for using search engines on the Internet. Also included are task definitions and key word worksheets.

# Search Strategy Worksheet

1.  What is your topic? _____

    _____

    _____

2.  What do you already know about your topic? _____

    _____

    _____

3.  List all the words or phrases you can think of that describe
    your topic. Consider synonyms, alternate spellings, techni-
    cal and everyday terms. _____

    _____

    _____

4.  List some questions that you want to answer. (What would
    you tell someone else about your topic?) _____

    _____

    _____

5.  Write a thesis statement that will define your topic and indi-
    cate the direction of your research. _____

    _____

    _____

6.  Identify the types of information you will be looking for.

    _____

    _____

7.  What resources will be the most useful to you? List these re-
    sources. _____

    _____

# Search Engines (Student Handout)

What is a Search Engine? Search Engines are computer programs that scan the content of servers on the World Wide Web, looking for keywords and search strings that you insert in a search box.

Each program may search for key words and search strings in various parts of a web site including its Title, URL, or Abstracts.

Search Engines vary in how searches are conducted. Some Search Engines permit advanced techniques known as Boolean Searching.

Before you begin your search, you must think out your search strategy.

Sometimes, spending some time thinking about your search will pay dividends in time saved on the Internet.

## SEARCH TIPS

1. It is always safer to use lower case letters to indicate a case insensitive match. If you type in any capital letters, you force an exact match on the entire word.

2. Use categories (when allowed) such as education, art, etc. for a more limited search.

3. Prioritize your terms and put the one with the greatest priority first in your search.

4. Using wildcards such as * (when allowed) permits you to expand your search.

5. Use more descriptive, specific words as opposed to general ones: "Lamborghini" instead of "Sports cars."

6. Identify synonyms or variations on words to help maximize results. For example: elderly people, senior citizens.

7. Search results are generally presented by listing the first ten on page one with a clickable option to see additional results on the next page.

8. Some Search Engines have pull down menus which allow you to target your search to The Web, News groups, News Wires, or URL's Summaries, Titles, etc.

9. Search results are generally sorted by relevance with the most relevant results nearest the top of the list.

10. Some Search Engines have a special "Related Topics" feature which allows you to locate additional resources in a similar area of interest.

Note: If information is more readily available and easier to access in a traditional resource, don't search for it on the Internet.

# Search Strategies Worksheet

Plan your search using Boolean logic:

1.  In a general sentence describe what you want to find on the Internet:

Example: To locate information about the food pyramid that young children can understand.

2.  From the above description, list the key concepts that you wish to search:

Example: Food pyramid, young children

3. List synonyms for each of the concepts described above:

Example:

| food pyramid | children | |
|---|---|---|
| nutrition | kids | |
| food groups | | |
| | | |

4.  Choose three of the following search engines and perform a comparative search:

| | |
|---|---|
| Lycos | www.lycos.com |
| Infoseek | www.infoseek.com |
| Webcrawler | webcrawler.com |
| Yahoo | www.yahoo.com |
| Altavista | altavista.digital.com |
| Excite | www.excite.com |

Search Engine

| 1. | 2. | 3. |
|---|---|---|
| Results | | |
| | | |
| | | |

Along with these worksheets or handouts is a listing of each of the search engines mentioned accompanied by information to access the specific tool, necessary rules to follow in order to be successful, and several examples of each operator and rule. These pages would prove to be useful for teachers and students alike. In addition, there are worksheets delineating the key word search process, requiring the student to think through the process thoroughly before beginning the search.

## Evaluating Information

A question that plagues every teacher and media specialist who works with Internet sources is: How does the student discern between reliable information on the Net and misinformation? Don Blake, senior technology analyst for the National Education Association's Center for Education Technology, states: "The most difficult challenge for the next generation will not be gaining access to information, but deciphering and discriminating among it—in other words, being information literate. . . . Preparing students for this overwhelming information flow is the difficult task facing educators" (Blake 1997).

Requiring the student to think through the search process before beginning the task is a good place to start in the process of managing information. The need to require assessment of the information gathered is also essential. The Carroll County document includes Kathy Schrock's "Guide for Educators: Critical Evaluation Survey; Secondary School Level" (http://www.capecod.net/schrockguide/evalhigh.htm). This is a three-page document that asks easy-to-answer questions about a completed Net search, including such topics as technical and visual aspects of the Web page, content, and authority and provides a space for a narrative evaluation. The authority piece is a particularly valuable section of the document; it queries authorship of the page, the organizations with which the author may be affiliated, whether or not the page has been reviewed by an online reviewing agency, what influence the domain of the page may have on the evaluation one makes, how the user can prove the information given is true, and whether the information is useful for the intended purpose and, if not, what steps can be taken next. A document such as this one will cause students to think twice before they accept the first hit in an information search, and most of all, will help them realize that everything found on the Internet is not necessarily factual.

Another assessment document developed by Carroll County (see p. 102) can be used during and after a project (either traditional or electronic) is being researched.

# Assessment of Research Activity
## Reference Interview

(Can be used as an assessment of how research is progressing and used to adopt changes in the assignment in the future.)

1. What is your topic?
2. What information have you been able to locate on your topic so far, for both print and nonprint?
3. What is the best information you have found? Why is it useful?
4. Is your topic too broad? Too narrow? How can you remedy this?
5. What key words have led you to the most useful information?
6. Is the information you found biased? Does the information support your hypothesis or thesis statement?
7. How up-to-date is the information? Is currency important for your topic? If you need more current data, where could you look?
8. Have you found illustrations, charts, or graphics to help you understand the topic?
9. How do you plan to present your findings? Do you need any of the production resources in the media center?
10. Are you comfortable using the library resources? Do you need additional instruction in the use of resources?

Interview may be signed by student and media specialist with appropriate comments.

Certainly all of the information presented so far in this chapter could be used with the English curriculum, but it could also be used with a research project that would be required anywhere in the school's curriculum. Carroll County specifically addresses English and library and information skills integration in a section of *High School Library Media Curriculum* entitled "English/Media Integration." In the introduction it states in part:

This booklet contains lessons which have been designed collaboratively by English teachers and the media specialist at Francis Scott Key High School. Some of the activities are presented in lesson plan format while others are in student assignment format. The implementation of these lessons was a cooperative venture between the classroom teacher and the media specialist. An additional purpose of this project is to increase communication between the English department and the Media Center by encouraging collaborative planning and cooperative teaching between the classroom teacher and the media specialist. Therefore, teachers and media specialists are encouraged to use these lessons as written or adapt them to serve different curriculum needs (Carroll County Public Schools 1997).

**Library Media and Drama 1**

The lesson shown is suggested for use with a Drama 1 class and uses the lesson plan format developed by the English department. The handouts for students are included just as they are written.

---

UNIT: Drama     LESSON: Career Research Assignment
Duration of Activity: 2 days

### Materials for Learning and Instruction:

Handouts:

- 1. Drama 1: Career Research Assignment
- 2. Note Taking Guidelines

### Class Outcomes:

Students will:

- 1. Research careers associated with the field of drama.
- 2. Use research skills to locate related information.
- 3. Access information found in the Media Center.

### Media Outcomes:

Students will:

- 1. List the key words associated with a chosen career.
- 2. Identify resources available for this activity.
- 3. Access information found in the Media Center.

### Assessment Items/Tasks That Will Be Used to Assess Achievement of Lesson Outcomes:

Students will:

- 1. List the key words associated with a chosen career.
- 2. Access a minimum of two sources to locate information.
- 3. Design and create a visual representation of chosen career based on notes.
- 4. Display and present career to the class.

### Assessment Criteria:

**Informal:** The teacher and media specialist will monitor and assess students' time on task during discussion and research. The teacher will monitor students' time on task during the students' presentations on careers.

**Formal:** The teacher will assess the research handouts for completion and quality of response. The teacher will assess the visual presentations for quality and creativity of response.

## Sequence of Lesson Activities and Approximate Time Frame:

Prior to going to the Media Center:

- The teacher introduces the assignment and instructs students to select a drama-related career to research on the following day.

### DAY 1.

1. The teacher reviews assignment and escorts students to the Media Center. (5 minutes)

2. The media specialist greets students and conducts a mini lesson on key words associated with careers. The students individually list the key words which relate to their topic. (5 minutes)

3. The media specialist introduces resources specific to the career field with which the students are not familiar. (5 minutes)

4. The students receive the handout for note taking and are instructed that these are the areas on which to take notes. (2 minutes)

5. The students access the available sources and record the found information on the theme handout. (35 minutes)

### DAY 2.

Students present the visual presentation of chosen career. (35 minutes)

> NOTE: The individual teacher can decide whether class time should be used for the creation of the visual presentation. This activity would work well in a four-module schedule as an activity concurrent with the practice of performance pieces.

# DRAMA 1: CAREER RESEARCH PROJECT
## (handout)

The world of drama has numerous career opportunities. Everyone that becomes involved with drama will not necessarily end up as the big movie or television star. There are numerous opportunities behind the scenes or even before performances begin.

Your assignment is to create some sort of visual representation of a career in the drama profession. After researching in the Media Center, you will design a sample project that is typical of the work in your chosen field. For example, if you choose to research in the field of design, you may choose to actually design a set for a specific play.

Here are the steps to use in completing this assignment.

1.  Choose a particular career in drama to research.

2.  Go to the library and find sources that provide information on that particular field.

3.  Design and create a visual representation of your chosen topic. Suggested topics include:

    | | |
    |---|---|
    | actor | electrical technician |
    | director | costume designer |
    | choreographer | makeup artist |
    | radio announcer | agent |
    | set designer | stunt person |

4.  Display or present your topic to the class.

# CAREER NOTE-TAKING HANDOUT

NATURE OF WORK:

WORKING CONDITIONS:

TRAINING, ADVANCEMENT, & QUALIFICATIONS:

JOB OUTLOOK & EARNINGS:

RELATED OCCUPATIONS:

---

From *Library Information Skills and the High School English Program*, 2nd ed. © 1999 Mary H. Hackman. Libraries Unlimited. (800) 237-6124.

All of the materials used in this lesson are included, and the media specialist, along with the English teacher, is encouraged to make any adjustments necessary to create a functional lesson for each school's instructional program. As feedback comes in, there will be alterations made to the original plan. When library and information skills are written into the district curriculum document in lesson plan format, there can be few acceptable reasons for not trying to integrate the two subject areas. It would be expected as media specialists and English teachers work together in implementing and adapting the lesson plans included in *High School Media Curriculum*, many additional plans will be developed at each high school media center and included in the guide for future use.

## Promoting Reading in Walkersville High School

In our world where emphasis upon "high tech" becomes the norm rather than the exception, it is refreshing to see media specialists—particularly at the high school level—still working toward encouraging students to appreciate literature. There remains the required reading done in the English classes, but all too often one hears: "But kids don't read for pleasure in high school." And in the midst of everything else the high school media specialist is expected to accomplish, it is the rare individual who makes the effort to motivate high school students to appreciate literature. One such media specialist is Kay Craig from Walkersville High School in Frederick County, Maryland. In addition to being a media specialist, she is an adjunct instructor in the library media graduate program at Western Maryland College; one of her subjects is Media Materials for Young Adults. Professionally, Craig must keep up with the available media in the field, and the Walkersville High School media center has an exemplary collection of young adult materials. Under Craig's direction, Rebecca Reickel, an English teacher in the high school and a library media program graduate student, completed a portion of a library media internship to fulfill the requirements for graduation. During the course of the internship, Reickel developed a lesson (see pp. 108–109) requiring her high school English students to explore a number of young adult novels and enabling them to check out the novels if they so desired. The lesson took place in one ninety-minute period with considerable work to be completed by the media specialist and/or English teacher beforehand.

# YOUNG ADULT NOVEL SURVEY

Library Media Skills Objectives:

>Students will read from books by various young adult authors.

>Students will choose books suited to their interests and reading levels.

>Students will provide feedback on the appeal of many young adult novels.

English Language Arts Objectives:

>Students will read novels independently.

>Students will determine the genre of various books.

>Students will informally evaluate the reading level of several young adult novels.

>Students will complete creative projects and share information about their novels.

Grade Level: Depending upon the books selected, this activity could be used with elementary students as well as high school students.

Resources:

>A sufficient number of good quality young adult novels to match or exceed the number of students in the targeted class.

Instructional Roles:

>The media specialist and the classroom teacher can share in the preparation of this lesson by selecting and marking short passages, one page or less, from each of the books to be used in the lesson.

>Either person can review different genres with the students and explain the activity.

>The classroom teacher will be responsible for assigning and evaluating the follow-up projects on the novels.

Activity and Procedures for Completion:

>Before the lesson begins, the media specialist and the classroom teacher should select from the library collection enough books to match or exceed the number of students in the classroom. The books should reflect the most popular young adult authors and cover different genres, with many realistic and suspense titles included. The instructors should place an index card in each book listing the author, title and

the page number of an interesting passage in the book; Post-It markers may be used to indicate the beginning of the passage in the book. (Appropriate adjustments may be made for students with limited cognitive or reading skills.)

In the media center, either the classroom teacher or the media specialist should review with the students the meaning of the term *genre* and generate a list of genres in fiction.

To begin the activity, each student will receive one marked book. The student should write on the response sheet the last name of the author and the title of the book. Next, the student should turn to the marked place and read the indicated passage. Each student will then try to determine the genre of the novel and include that on the sheet. Students will also indicate the number of pages in the book and the reading level (according to their personal judgment) as Easy, Medium or Difficult; finally they should give the book one to three stars for appeal based upon the passage read (one star is the least appealing; three stars is the most appealing).

When students have accomplished this task and questions have been answered by the classroom teacher and the media specialist, they will trade books and repeat the process. The books will have been arranged so that students will see a variety of genres in the books they receive. One easy way to do this is to group the books in sets of four, five or six, depending on the number of students seated at one library table and have the students pass the books around as they finish until they have read from each one. The amount of time it will take to do this and the number of passes they can sustain depends upon the age and level of the class. The objectives of this assignment can be achieved even if each student evaluates only four or five books, but eight to ten books will give a broader view.

At the conclusion of this activity, students select books for independent reading. They should be encouraged to share information and look for other books in the genres and by the authors they found appealing.

Evaluation:

When students have finished the independent reading of their selected novels, they will complete creative projects related to the books. Posters, Book Covers, Three-Dimensional Scenes, Puppets, Journals, Photography Displays, Live Performances and Videos are possible suggestions.

Follow-up:

Students will present their projects to the class (Reickel 1997).

(This activity is accompanied by a response sheet that includes the information requested for each book examined: Author's last name, Title, Genre, Readability, Number of Pages and Evaluation by Number of Stars.)

It should be noted that when this lesson was completed successfully with one class, adjustments were made for the next class assigned the activity. For example, some titles were substituted for existing ones when members of the first class expressed a definite dislike for a title (much too easy, much too hard, read this in seventh grade, etc.). There is every reason to assume the activity will change each time it is taught in the future; that is expected in good teaching. Plans are adjusted to fit the student and accommodate available resources.

In the examples given in this chapter, one can readily see that the possibilities are many when some effort is made to integrate the two disciplines, the English curriculum, and library media skills. Whether the classroom teacher or the media specialist is teaching information skills or motivating the student to read for enjoyment, the task should be made easier to accomplish and more effective in its delivery if the two work together.

 ## Resources for Library Media Specialists for Teaching Library and Information Skills

Barron, Ann E., and Gary W. Orwig. 1997. *New Technologies for Education: A Beginner's Guide.* Third Edition. Littleton, Colo.: Libraries Unlimited.

Barron, Ann E., and Karen S. Ivers. 1996. *The Internet and Instruction: Activities and Ideas.* Littleton, Colo.: Libraries Unlimited.

California Media and Library Educators Association. 1994. *From Library Skills to Information Literacy: A Handbook for the 21st Century.* Castle Rock, Colo.: Hi Willow Research.

Campbell, D., and M. Campbell. 1995. *The Student's Guide to Doing Research on the Internet.* Reading, Mass.: Addison-Wesley.

Desberg, Peter, and Farah Fisher. 1995. *Teaching with Technology.* 4 Macintosh disks. Des Moines, Iowa: Allyn & Bacon.

Eisenberg, Michael B., and Robert E. Berkowitz. 1990. *Information Problem Solving: The Big Six Skills™ Approach to Library and Information Skills Instruction.* Norwood, N. J.: Ablex.

Ellsworth, J. H. 1994. *Education on the Internet: A Hands-On Book of Ideas, Projects and Advice.* Indianapolis, Ind.: Sams.

Farmer, Lesley J. 1995. *Workshops for Teachers: Becoming Partners for Information Literacy.* Worthington, Ohio: Linworth.

Grabe, Mark, and Cindy Grabe. 1996. *Integrating Technology for Meaningful Learning.* Wilmington, Mass.: Houghton Mifflin.

Junion-Metz, G. 1996. *K–12 Resources on the Internet: An Instructional Guide.* Berkeley, Calif.: Library Solutions Press.

Le Baron, John F., Catherine Collier, and Linda de Lyon Friel. 1996. *A Travel Agent In Cyberschool: The Internet and the Library Media Program.* Littleton, Colo.: Libraries Unlimited.

Libutti, Patricia O'Brien. 1995. *Teaching Information Retrieval and Evaluation Skills to Education Students and Practitioners: A Casebook of Applications.* Chicago: ALA.

Mandrinos, Roxanne. 1994. *Building Information Literacy Using High Technology: A Guide for Schools and Libraries.* Littleton, Colo.: Libraries Unlimited.

Ryba, Rich. 1995. *Power Teaching: How to Develop Creative Teaching Techniques Using CD-ROM Technology to Supercharge Your Classroom.* Video, 25 minutes. Sheffield, Mass.: Educational Reform Group.

Simpson, C. M. 1995. *Internet for Library Media Specialists.* Worthington, Ohio: Linworth.

Strichart, Stephen S. 1997. *Study Skills and Strategies for High School Students in the Information Age: Ready-to-Use Reproducible Activities.* New York: Allyn & Bacon.

Valmont, William J. 1995. *Creating Videos for School Use.* New York: Allyn & Bacon.

Volkman, John D. 1998. *Cruising Through Research and Library Skills for Young Adults.* Littleton, Colo.: Libraries Unlimited.

Yuedt, Alice H. 1997. *Flip It! Information Literacy Skills.* Worthington, Ohio: Linworth.

# Chapter 9

## Shakespeare

What is taught and what is not taught in the realm of literature in the English curriculum frequently depends upon the emphasis of the times. Certainly there are many brilliant works of literature from which to choose in order to satisfy a particular outcome in an English course. Earlier in this book, there was mention of the pendulum in education that swings from the zenith to the nadir and back again if one is around long enough. This writer remembers taking a college course in the 1950s in Twentieth Century American Writers and being told that F. Scott Fitzgerald was successful in his time but was a "flash in the pan" in reality. English teachers did not use Fitzgerald, as a rule, when teaching American literature in the 1950s and 1960s, but in the 1970s and 1980s Fitzgerald was back in vogue, and his books still appear in many curriculum documents. Needless to say, most secondary school library media collections have enough copies of his work to satisfy the demand.

The one author who seems untouched by the pendulum swings and who has probably been included as part of the English curriculum since curriculum was first created is William Shakespeare. If one were to take a look at the current *Books in Print*, one would see that there are a number of works with recent dates concerning the Bard of Avon. The same is true with regard to theatrical productions of Shakespeare's plays; his plays are being performed on stage and in films throughout the world. Scarcely a season goes by without several Shakespearean works being performed in regional and/or community theaters in the United States. The Internet is another source in the modern world for access to Shakespeare, with many sites available, including his complete works. It is obvious, then, that Shakespeare is not subject to elimination from an English course of study just because his works were not created in the modern day. From the Sixteenth century, he has managed to address the emotions and the intellect of contemporary audiences with an art that transcends time.

With this rationale, let us "brush up on our Shakespeare" in terms of library media skills and strategies that can be integrated into the English program. In selecting Shakespeare to use as an example for integrating media and English, it is important to remember that many of his plays are suitable to be read by high school students. Also, his plays are often performed at the high school level. It is my belief that every student should have the opportunity to be exposed to this literary giant by whatever means possible. There was a time when only the college-bound student read Shakespeare as part of his or her English curriculum—sometimes, this is still the rule. The college-bound student will have further opportunities to expand those literary horizons; the student who will leave high school and go directly into the world of work may not have the good fortune to learn about and savor these plays.

Today's students have many chances to see Shakespearean production, whatever the medium. I recall being taken to Ford's Theatre in Baltimore by my high school English teachers to see such great actors as Maurice Evans and Judith Anderson portray Shakespeare's characters—experiences that left an indelible impression upon the heart and mind. These plays were written to be performed, not just read. Both English teachers and media specialists must keep in mind that in Shakespeare's day, the vast majority of the audience at the Globe Theatre was illiterate, and apparently the subtleties and the twists of plot were understood and applauded. Today's students can see a play, film, made-for-television production, or musical adaptation of one of Shakespeare's plays, then use the Internet for further information, listen to a cassette tape, and even select a role to play while interacting with a CD-ROM programmed to permit this activity. The list goes on, but genuine understanding comes when the student has the chance to learn with his or her peers about the author, his time, and his works.

 ## Romeo and Juliet

While there are many plays from which to choose, *Romeo and Juliet* seems to speak loudly and clearly to adolescents. Much that is relevant to today's teenager is there: a love story culminating in a secret marriage, families who do not get along with other families, intrigue and conspiracy on the part of a well-meaning friar, parents who do not understand their adolescent offspring, suicide, and guilt. Teenage marriage, violence in our society, and suicide are all subjects that high school students frequently select when writing research papers on contemporary issues. The spin-offs from this play are many and appear in a variety of art forms. The continuing popularity of *West Side Story* speaks to the appeal that a modern, musical version of *Romeo and Juliet* holds for young people, as well as adults.

For the purpose of this chapter, then, *Romeo and Juliet* is the play that will be used to demonstrate activities that can be implemented jointly by the English teacher and the library media specialist. (It does not matter which of Shakespeare's plays is used. The ideas are interchangeable in general terms.)

Karen Marcus writes in an issue of the *English Journal* about her experience in working with special needs students and "found that Shakespeare texts can help and heal adolescents who are in remedial high school classes" (Marcus 1996). She participated in a training institute originally designed for actors from Shakespeare and Company, a theater company from Lenox, Massachusetts. This program involved training in movement, voice, and text; Marcus utilized the skills she learned when she returned to her high school English classroom. After Marcus edited the text of *Romeo and Juliet*, her students were given the chance to become the characters, keep journals about those characters and complete several intriguing movement and writing exercises. "Students become characters, create settings or embody key words. This is just one avenue to success because it involves cooperative learning, stressing group effort and spirit. The by-product is that the students have fun with their peers while studying Shakespeare" (Marcus 1996). Of course they had fun. They had a teacher who took the time to ply her recently learned editing skills to make *Romeo and Juliet* a comfortable vehicle for her students to use, worked with her students on movement and voice techniques, and encouraged them to get to know their characters intimately. This would have been one of those unforgettable high school experiences for these students. If the teacher is willing and able to make the effort and take the time, the learning level of the students in the class is not important when it comes to teaching Shakespeare.

There are a number of areas where the library media specialist can take an active part in teaching the information skills needed for an English project involving Shakespeare. In addition to exposing students to Shakespeare's rich language, singular characters, and intricate plots, the lesson should give them a grasp of Shakespeare, the man, and the time in which he lived and wrote. Students need to know about his Elizabethan contemporaries and the audiences that attended the Globe Theatre. One of the questions that frequently comes from the student who is reading Shakespeare (or seeing a production) is, "Why does he write so weird?" They need to know about the English language and the morality of that time. This kind of information is usually a prelude to the actual reading or viewing of the play. One sets the stage, so to speak. There are undoubtedly as many ways of approaching the study of Shakespeare's background as there are teachers of English. Whatever method is chosen, the media specialist should be an important part of the endeavor.

 # Lesson Plan for Shakespearean Study

---

Background information about Shakespeare and the Elizabethan Era....

## English/Language Arts Outcomes
The student will:

- Select a topic to research from a list of topics.
- Develop an outline for reporting on the topic selected.
- Locate at least three sources on the topic (one source must be an electronic source and one must be a traditional source).
- Upon completing the research, prepare an oral presentation on the topic using appropriate media.
- Synthesize the flavor of the Elizabethan period from hearing and/or viewing peer presentations.

## Library and Information Skills Outcomes

The student will:

- Use components of research strategies to evaluate, select, record and reorganize information.
- Explore a variety of sources for information purposes.
- Recognize the impact of technology on information.
- Discriminate among various types of media to produce the appropriate medium for a particular purpose.

Time Frame:

Three ninety-minute periods or six fifty-five-minute periods will be required to complete the research and present the project (depending upon class levels).

Suggested Topics (Students may add to the list with teacher approval.):

- The Globe Theatre (in Elizabethan times and present day)
- Productions of Shakespeare's plays in Elizabethan times
- Shakespeare's audiences
- Elizabeth 1 and her court
- Life of Shakespeare, including his acting career
- Elizabethan authors (Ben Johnson, Christopher Marlowe, etc.)
- The Black Plague and Elizabethan health care
- Sources of Shakespeare's plays and Elizabethan English language
- Costumes in Shakespeare's plays (Elizabethan times and today)
- Actors in Elizabethan times, especially in Shakespeare's plays
- A day in the life of an Elizabethan family
- An overview of the world during Queen Elizabeth's reign
- Commerce and trade in Elizabethan England

Resources:

Library media catalog, encyclopedias, indexes, bibliographies, CD-ROMs, appropriate Internet and Web sites, production equipment and materials—transparencies, audiocassettes, videotapes, pens, markers, paints, computer disks, appropriate computer programs such as Power Point, etc.

Activity:

This activity is divided into three parts. The class will be introduced to the study of Shakespeare's *Romeo and Juliet* and to this project by the teacher. The English teacher will divide the class into small groups consisting of no more than three students each. Each group will decide which topic will be researched and prepare subject heading and key word search strategies for the media center visit. This is an important step because if the Internet is being used, students will find many hits and the need to narrow the search and carefully read the given information is paramount to eventual success as the research continues.

# Part 1.

The library media specialist will give a brief overview of the available resources and make suggestions as to the subject heading and key word searches when the class comes to the media center. Students will need to know what the possibilities are for production as they begin their research and perhaps tailor the organization of their project to fit a specific format. The first part of the allotted time will be spent locating and evaluating appropriate resources, then writing an outline and organizing and compiling the information for the selected topic. When the information has been compiled and the students are ready to move to the next phase, each group will decide what medium it will use to present the information gathered to the class and the students will use the production equipment on a first come, first served basis. In addition to providing individual help with production, the media specialist will have prepared a step-by-step direction sheet for each process to assure good results with every project. Homework can be assigned for the compilation part of the assignment as appropriate.

# Part 2.

The students will go to the media center to complete the written part of the project and begin to work on the production phase. The teacher and the media specialist will work with each group as they complete this portion of the assignment. There will be time allotted for practicing the projects prior to the actual presentations.

# Part 3.

The oral presentations will take place in the media center or the classroom depending upon the facilities available. The media specialist and the teacher will be involved in the evaluation of the projects, as appropriate.

Evaluation:

| | |
|---|---|
| Resources used | 25 points |
| Organization | 25 points |
| Production | 25 points |
| Presentation | 25 points |

The media specialist could assign the points earned for resources and production and the English teacher could assign the points earned for organization and presentation.

Follow-up:

Both the media specialist and the teacher should examine the results of the project and determine ways to improve upon it for the next time it is assigned. Were resources adequate? Did students have enough time to complete the assignment? Were the presentations successful in terms of the desired outcomes?

---

There are many ways in which the study of Shakespeare in the English class can be integrated into information and library skills instruction. Students can research the various productions in contemporary times, as well as the earliest recorded productions from times past then look at critical writings, publicity techniques, alterations made to the original scripts, and the actors who played the various roles. They can examine the setting for a play and complete an information search of the time and place in which the play is set to see if there are correlations with the plot and the actual history of the place. Web pages can be developed by students to expose their findings to others who may be interested in the same subject. Web pages may exist where the student can write a letter to any one of many Shakespearean characters and receive a reply in the guise of that character. Parts of plays can be learned and performed for other classes or televised and recorded for many uses. The journal idea illustrated in the unit developed by Karen Marcus is an excellent one to use with students. The student assumes the role of one of the characters and keeps a journal of that character's thoughts and feelings.

It should not be difficult to find a professional or a community theater production of a Shakespearean play or of an adaptation in a local theater for students to see and compare the live experience with reading the play. The comparison of film versions of many of Shakespeare's plays with the written word is an interesting assignment and provides the opportunity for greater understanding of the writer's work. A further scrutiny of the personalities who made history in the Elizabethan era would be worthwhile as one looks at the words Shakespeare used to describe England, such as a unique "sceptered isle" and a "seat of Mars." Why was the Elizabethan age referred to in history books as the "golden age of the Empire?"

The projects are endless and every teacher and media specialist who has taught Shakespeare could add many, many more ideas. The point is, of course, to expose students to this playwright and the multitude of resources available about him and the period in which he wrote. And formats are such that students of almost any level can have the opportunity to enjoy Shakespeare.

 ## Suggested Resources for Shakespeare Study

Search the Net! There are hundreds of entries that relate to the study of Shakespeare and *Romeo and Juliet* specifically. A sampling of addresses that may prove to be helpful and were available as of December 12, 1997, are:

Complete Works of Shakespeare
- http://www.the-tech.mit.edu/shakespeare.html

DeCaprio's *Romeo and Juliet* (the famous film depicting the play)
- http://www.movieweb.com/movie/romeojuliet/index

Romeo and Juliet's Fair Verona (write to and receive letters from the play's characters)
- http://www.geocities.com

Shakespeare A to Z: The Essential Reference to His Plays, His Poems, His Life and Times, and More
- http://www.lib.ua.edu/shakie3.htm

Shakespeare Alive! (resource materials for teaching Shakespeare)
- http://www.kadets.d29.co.chu/shakespeare/shaktch.html

Shakespeare and his Contemporaries (biographical information on Shakespeare and his peers)
- http://www.bcpl.lid.md.us/~tross/ws/oy3.html

Shakespeare Resources (includes electronic sites on the Globe Theater, Stratford on Avon, online texts, lesson plans, and bibliographies)
- http://falcon.jmu.edu/"/shakes.htm

Shakespearean Homework Helper (general information on the man and his works)
- http://shakespeare.htm@members.aol.com

#  Traditional Resources for Studying Shakespeare

Bate, Jonathan, and Russell Jackson, editors. 1996. *Shakespeare: An Illustrated Stage History.* New York: Oxford University Press.

Berry, Ralph. 1989. *On Directing Shakespeare: Interviews with Contemporary Directors.* London: Hamish Hamilton.

———. 1993. *Shakespeare in Performance: Castings and Metamorphoses.* New York: St. Martin's Press.

Boyce, Charles. 1991. *Shakespeare A to Z: The Essential Reference to His Plays, His Life and Times, and More.* New York: Dell.

Crowl, Samuel. 1992. *Shakespeare Observed: Studies in Performance on Stage and Screen.* Athens, Ohio: Ohio University Press.

DeVere, Rollin. 1993. *A Hawk from a Handsaw: A Student's Guide to the Shakespeare Mystery.* Hunting Valley, Ohio: University School Press.

*Editions and Adaptations of Shakespeare.* 1996. Alexandria, Va.: Chadwyck-Healey. CD-ROM for Windows.

Kay, Dennis. 1995. *William Shakespeare: His Life and Times.* New York: Scribner Reference.

Kennedy, Dennis. 1993. *Looking at Shakespeare: A Visual History of Twentieth Century Performance.* New York: Cambridge University Press.

Lace, William W. 1995. *Elizabethan England.* San Diego, Calif.: Lucent Books.

Levi, Peter. 1995. *The Life and Times of William Shakespeare.* New York: Random House.

Ogburn, Charlton. 1995. *The Man Who Was Shakespeare: A Summary of the Case Unfolded in the Mysterious William Shakespeare, the Myth and the Reality.* McLean, Va.: EPM Publications.

Richmond, Hugh, producer. 1985. *Shakespeare and the Globe.* Berkeley, Calif.: University of California. Video cassette, 31 minutes.

*Romeo and Juliet: Center Stage.* 1996. Pleasantville, N.Y.: Sunburst. CD-ROM with sound, graphics, text, movies, videotapes, and teacher's guide for Macintosh.

Sammartino, Peter. 1990. *The Man Who Was William Shakespeare.* New York: Cornwall.

*Shakespeare Is Alive and Well in the Modern World.* 1990. Mount Kisco, N.Y.: Center for the Humanities. Video cassette, 45 minutes.

*Shakespeare's World.* 1983. Monmence, Ill.: distributed by Baker and Taylor. Video cassette, three-part documentary including *Shakespeare's Country, Shakespeare's Stratford,* and *Shakespeare's Heritage*, 30 minutes each.

*Shakespeare: Time Quest.* 1994. New York: The Cinema Guild. Video cassette, 21 minutes.

# Chapter 10

## "To-morrow, and to-morrow, and to-morrow . . ."

The American Library Association gives us statistics that cite the number of libraries of all kinds in the United States. Figures from 1994–1995 indicate there are 97,976 school library media centers, and chances are good those numbers are growing. We enter the year 2000, then, with close to 100,000 school library media centers in this country. The total number of libraries listed in this source is 122,663, and that number includes public libraries (8,929), academic libraries (3,274), special libraries (10,192), armed forces libraries (428), and government libraries (1,864). The number of public libraries skews the total figure because the count given includes only the administrative units; when one counts the branches of the central administrative buildings, the total number of public libraries reaches 15,946 (ALA 1997). The obvious fact is that there are many more school library media centers than all other kinds of libraries put together. And, this is a fact that should make library media professionals, and educators in general, very much aware of the responsibilities that are part and parcel of a library and information skills program.

What of the quality of the program delivered in those 97,976 library media centers? Does even having a media center in a school make a difference in the progress made by the students? What steps can be taken to make programs more vital and media specialists seen as active and enthusiastic members of the teaching staff, knowledgeable about learning styles and instructional design? How does the media specialist keep up with the latest developments in information technology and continue to provide instruction in the use of current technology to teachers and students alike? How important is a public relations program, and how much time can be devoted to it? And, speaking of time, what is the obligation of the high school media specialist when it comes to promoting reading as a leisure-time activity? How important are memberships and participation in professional organizations?

Of course, this list of queries could go on and on, but the answer is almost always the same. It depends upon the media specialist. Provisions can be made by supervisors for inservice training in new technologies; ideas can be shared for lessons, media program promotions, curriculum development, encouraging young adult reading, integrating library and information skills into the curriculum, and even ways of getting it all organized; but when one gets to the bottom line, it is the media specialist and the attitude, as well as the knowledge, with which he or she approaches the job that truly matters. Enthusiasm is catching, and teachers, students, administrators, and parents react to it in a positive fashion. The library media specialist needs to be enthusiastic in the approach taken to the job, no matter the lack of funding or time or assistance. This does not mean that those who can provide funding, time, and assistance should not be given the information necessary to make a good argument for those things needed to make the media program a better one. It does mean that subject area teachers do not need to see the media specialist as a complainer or as one who does the job grudgingly. Time needs to be organized so that it is spent with students and teachers, not operating the circulation desk or checking in new materials during those periods when the media specialist is in demand. Indeed,

the job is never done and that fact should be part of the understanding when one enters the field of school librarianship.

The good news is that library media programs in schools do make a difference and a positive one. In the *School Library Media Quarterly*, Ken Haycock writes that students in schools with good library media centers do considerably better in a variety of tests than their counterparts who lack these services. He indicates that students read more and enjoy it more when their school has a media center and a library media specialist. There can be little doubt that students learn more and enjoy it more when they have a knowledgeable and enthusiastic media specialist team with their English teacher to teach information skills as they begin to do research for a term paper. Haycock also points to the institutions responsible for training media specialists where there needs to be a greater emphasis on "cooperative program planning and teaching and the skills necessary to convince educators that library media specialists are vital partners in instruction" (Haycock 1995).

No one has the ability to look into the future definitively. With the rapid developments occurring in the world of computer technology, one cannot help but wonder what lies ahead. And, it seems as though everyone has an opinion. During a recent visit to the dentist, I was asked in a somewhat playful manner, "Don't you really think libraries are things of the past? How much longer do you think we'll have books?" (Questions guaranteed to make a not very pleasant situation even more unpleasant.) The response was simple and perhaps unfair because it was in the form of a question: "Do you have children?" There was a long hesitation before he said, "Yes, I do. And I see your point. I want them to read books and to love reading. I guess it would be a sad world without libraries. But, I want them to be savvy about technology too. Can you do all of that?" The answer this time was: "We try. And we don't try to do it alone." The conversation stopped as the dentist concentrated on his work and rendered my mouth incapable of further speech. Can there be any doubt that it would be a sad world without libraries? And where would the school media specialist be if he or she tried to fulfill all expectations without enormous cooperation from teachers, parents, and administrators?

In March 1997, a presentation was made to Maryland's state superintendent of schools, Dr. Nancy Grasmick, on the subject of school library media programs. The presenter was A. Brian Helm, director of Library Services in Anne Arundel County, Maryland. In cooperation with Gail Bailey, Chief of the School Library Media Services Branch at the Maryland State Department of Education, and at the request of the state school board, Helm stepped into his role as a member of the Maryland Advisory Council on Libraries, under whose auspices he made his presentation. His words speak directly to that tomorrow which is surely coming.

# Information Literacy—The New Basic

Maryland Advisory Council on Libraries
Thursday, March 20, 1997
Presentation to Dr. Nancy Grasmick
Library Media Programs

## The Shared Roles of Libraries

Libraries of all types have a crucial responsibility for promoting the information literacy skills of all individuals in the State of Maryland. School library media centers and public, academic, and special libraries must work aggressively and cooperatively to provide children and adults with the skills to locate, evaluate, and use information effectively to solve problems and enhance their lives.

Cooperation between libraries is essential because libraries share several core goals: (1) Providing access to information resources; (2) ensuring that students and adults are effective users of information; and (3) motivating children, young adults, and adults to use library materials for both recreational and informational needs. These goals are directed at assuring an information literate society.

Media centers and libraries of tomorrow will provide students with network connections within the school (intranet), from the home, and in libraries. Access to information resources (text, graphic, and motion media) will become increasingly seamless. Libraries foster information literacy, independent learning, and social responsibility.

Information literacy is therefore fundamental to citizenship education— a common goal shared by all libraries.

## The Changing Role of the Library Media Specialist and Library Media Center in Fostering Information Literacy

Harnessing the power of technology requires our students to become skilled information problem-solvers and to use basic skills of deciphering, producing, and exchanging information in commonly accepted and clearly understood language. Media specialists seek to cultivate a healthy skepticism in students by promoting their skills in questioning, judging, making distinctions, and recognizing motives and techniques.

Information literacy is the ability to choose, to understand, to question, to evaluate, to create or produce, and to respond thoughtfully to the information that we consume. Students must possess the ability to make judgments, compare and contrast, critique, and apply ethics; they must be able to communicate in a variety of formats to different audiences.

The changing role of the media specialist is increasingly focused on collaboration with teachers and other librarians to facilitate learning and provide information services to learners wherever they are. In promoting information literacy, the media specialist concentrates on processes rather than content and seeks to develop students who are competent, independent learners. Information literate students can identify information needs and actively engage in the world of ideas. They can identify relevant information and solve problems. They manage technology tools to access information and to communicate. Information literate students adapt easily to change and work well in groups. The qualities of the information literate student are the same qualities that all libraries seek to promote in their patrons. As a result of becoming information literate, our students and citizens will be able to answer the questions and deal with the problems that occur daily. Information literate individuals are students who create quality products. They are young adults capable of analyzing job opportunities and parents capable of making informed decisions regarding the future or well being of their children. They include older citizens who are informed consumers able to ask probing questions about the reliability and validity of commercial offers. Information literate students and community members have the ability to ask questions about difficult problems and work toward solutions as a group. Information literate individuals have the ability to gather information to solve problems such as violence, pollution, or child care needs. Students who are information literate will become the next generation of community leaders and cultural influencers.

Library media specialists are in the important position of simultaneously providing access to and instruction in the use of technological information resources and traditional print information resources. They skillfully maintain a critical balance by promoting the value of all information resources while teaching skills in their effective use.

The school library media specialist provides instructional programs that teach information literacy skills that require problem-solving and critical thinking in all subjects in grades K–12. Partnerships are established with public and academic libraries in this endeavor with the goal of enabling students to become independent life-long learners.

Information literacy will be an essential survival skill in the twenty-first century. Students will need to achieve a higher degree of information literacy as information sources proliferate. The media specialist provides students with skills in (1) acquiring appropriate information, (2) organizing and applying information at appropriate times, and, (3) using information effectively with others. Acquiring information entails thinking skills—classifying, interpreting, analyzing, summarizing, synthesizing, and evaluating information. Using information requires the fostering of cooperative skills in groups. In this context it is impossible to imagine how teachers will truly advance information literacy without access to and use of the school library media center. Students cannot become information literate in any subject area through the use of a single information resource.

## Challenges

Initiatives related to the promotion of information literacy in school library media programs face several challenges. In order to fulfill their role effectively, media specialists need regular staff development training to upgrade their skills in accessing information, using technology, teaching with technology, and providing staff development training for teachers in the use of technology.

Media programs must be provided with adequate funding for information resources to ensure equity throughout Maryland. Rapidly increasing demands brought about by the infusion of technology has frequently stretched existing staff to the limits in terms of their ability to provide information resources, resource services, and instruction in the use of these resources. Adequate staffing must be provided if library media specialists are expected to meet the demands of their rapidly changing role.

The rapid expansion of new technologies is delivering an immense quantity of information and new implications for its use. As educators, the library community must harness the power of emerging technologies like the Internet, but we must also play "catch up." Television, telephone, and computer technology are merging and becoming even more pervasive and more powerful. We cannot afford to observe these changes passively and thereby allow commercial, conflicting, or even negative trends to be the only or primary determining factors of our children's literacy achievement.

Unless schools respond adequately to the integration of technology into education, students will increasingly view their education as irrelevant. The library media center plays a critical role in this integration (Helm 1997).

---

We do know that school media specialists will continue to provide students and teachers with books and other media for enjoyment or for specific information purposes. One can hope that there will be favorable responses to arguments such as the foregoing one and that adequate funding, staffing, and technology will become the norm rather than the exception. It becomes more and more important to integrate library and information skills with all curricula because that leads to meaningful information literacy. One would like to be certain that students and those who teach them have the opportunity to become information literate and know, without a doubt, that they have been served well by school library media specialists.

# Appendix A

 **Associations for School Library Media and English Personnel**

### American Association of School Librarians (AASL)
50 East Huron Street
Chicago, IL 60611

> Publications: *School Library Media Quarterly*
> * *Hot Line Connections*
>
> Meetings: Annual Conference with ALA
> * Mid-Winter Meeting with ALA
> * Bi-Annual Convention

### American Library Association (ALA)
50 East Huron Street
Chicago, IL 60611

> Publications: *American Libraries*
> * *Booklist*
> * *Book Links*
> * *Choice*
>
> Meetings: Annual Conference
> * Mid-Winter Meeting

### American Society for Educators (ASE)
1429 Walnut Street
Philadelphia, PA 19102

> Publications: *Media and Methods*

### Association for Supervision and Curriculum Development (ASCD)
1250 Pitt Street
Alexandria, VA 22314

> Publications: *ASCD Yearbook*
> * *Curriculum Update*
> * *Education*
>
> Meetings: Annual Conference

### Association for Educational Communications and Technology (AECT)

1025 Vermont Avenue, NW
Suite 820
Washington, DC 20005

Publications: *Tech Trends*
- *Educational Technology Research and Development*
- *Report to Members*

Meetings: Annual Conference and INCITE Exposition

### Computer Using Educators (CUE)

1210 Marina Village Parkway
Suite 100
Alameda, CA 94501
E-mail: cueinc@aol.com

Publications: *CUE Newsletter*

Meetings: Spring and Fall Conferences

### International Reading Association (IRA)

800 Barksdale Road
P. O. Box 8139
Newark, DE 19714

Publications: *Journal of Adolescent and Adult Reading*
- *Reading Research Quarterly*
- *Reading Today*

Meetings: Annual Convention
- Biennial Adolescent/Adult Literary Conference

### National Council of Teachers of English (NCTE)

1111 Kenyon Road
Urbana, IL 61801

Publications: *College English*
- *English Education*
- *English Journal*
- *English Leadership Quarterly*
- *Language Arts*
- *Voices from the Middle*

Meetings: Annual Conference

# References Cited

Aftab, Parry. 1997. *A Parents' Guide to the Internet: And How to Protect Your Children in Cyberspace.* Paramus, N. J.: S.C. Press.

American Association of School Librarians (AASL) and the Association for Educational Communication and Technology (AECT). 1975. *Media Programs: District and School.* Chicago: American Library Association.

————. 1988. *Information Power: Guidelines for School Library Media Programs.* Chicago: American Library Association.

American Association of School Librarians (AASL) and the Department of Audio Visual Instruction of the National Education Association (DAVI). 1969. *Standards for School Media Programs.* Chicago: American Library Association.

American Library Association. LARC Fact Sheet #1. http://www.ala.org/library/factl/html (Accessed December 1997).

Anne Arundel County Public Schools. 1997. *Library Media Instructional Program.* Revised. Annapolis, Md.: Anne Arundel County Public Schools.

Baltimore County Public Schools. 1997. *Indicators of Learning: English—Grades 9, 10, and 11.* Towson, Md.: Baltimore County Public Schools.

————. 1998a. *Baltimore County Public Facts 1998–99.* Towson, Md.: Baltimore County Public Schools, Office of Communications and Special Projects.

————. 1998b. *Parent Internet Education, Unit 1—Internet Issues: Understanding the Spirit of the Internet—Why Evaluate?* Towson, Md.: Baltimore County Public Schools.

Beauchamp, George. 1983. *Curriculum Design—Fundamental Curriculum Decisions.* Edited by Fenwick English. Alexandria, Va.: Association of Supervision and Curriculum Development, 1983 Yearbook Committee.

Biggs, Mary. 1979. Foreword to Basics in Library Instruction. *School Library Journal* 14 (5): 44.

Blake, Don. 1997. Web Report Card. *Yahoo* 3 (September): 58.

Brickell, William. 1975. Speech Before Maryland Library Media Specialists, October, Annapolis, Md.

Carroll County Public Schools. 1997. *High School Library Media Curriculum.* Westminster, Md.: Library Media Services, Carroll County Public Schools.

Eisenberg, Michael, and Robert Berkowitz. 1989. *Information Problem Solving: The Big-Six Skills™ Approach to Library and Information Skills Instruction.* Norwood, N.J.: Ablex.

Haycock, Ken. 1995. Research in Teacher-Librarianship and the Institutionalization of Change. *School Library Media Quarterly* 23 (4): 227–33.

Helm, A. Brian. 1997. "Information Literacy—The New Basic." Speech before Dr. Nancy Grasmick, Maryland Superintendent of Schools, and the Maryland State Board of Education, March, Baltimore, Md.

Hicks, Warren B. 1981. *Managing the Building-Level School Library Media Program.* Chicago: American Library Association.

Howard County Public Schools. 1997. *The Essential Curriculum Documents: English 8-9.* Pilot Copy. Ellicott City, Md.: Howard County Public Schools.

Lally, Kathy. *Centennial High: Top of the Class. Part 3.* "Lives Defined by the Paper." *Baltimore Sun* (June 17, 1997): A-1, 6.

Marcus, Karen. 1996. All You Need Is Love: Using Shakespeare to Build Community. *English Journal* (3): 58–60.

Maryland State Department of Education. 1987. *Standards for School Library Media Programs in Maryland.* Baltimore, Md.: Maryland State Department of Education, School Library Media Services Branch.

———. 1991. *Library Media Program: A Maryland Curricular Framework.* Baltimore, Md.: Maryland State Department of Education, School Library Media Services Branch.

———. 1994. *Learning Outcomes in Library Media Skills.* Baltimore, Md.: Maryland State Department of Education, School Library Media Services Branch.

———. 1996. *High School Core Learning Goals for the English Program.* Baltimore, Md.: Maryland State Department of Education, Language Development and Early Learning Branch.

National Council of Teachers of English (NCTE) and International Reading Association (IRA). 1996. *Standards for the English Language Arts.* Urbana, Ill.: NCTE.

National Study of School Evaluation (NSSE). 1987. *Evaluative Criteria for the Evaluation of Secondary Schools,* 6th edition. Falls Church, Va.: National Study of School Evaluation.

———. 1997. *Indicators of Schools of Quality. Schoolwide Indicators of Quality.* Vol. 1. Schaumburg, Ill.: National Study of School Evaluation.

Pawlowski, Connie, and Patsy Troutman. 1995. Blending Print and Electronic Sources. *Library Research Skills: Grades 7-12,* 2nd edition. Worthington, Ohio: Linworth Publishing, 50–51.

Reickel, Rebecca. 1997. *Lesson Plan: Young Adult Novel Survey.* Walkersville, Md.: Walkersville High School, Frederick County Public Schools.

Walker, Thomas, and Paula Kay Montgomery. 1977. *Teaching Media Skills: An Instructional Program for Elementary and Middle School Students.* Littleton, Colo.: Libraries Unlimited.

Washington County Public Schools. 1994. *Washington County Library Media Essential Curriculum.* Draft copy. Hagerstown, Md.: Office of Library Media Services, Washington County Public Schools.

# Index